A WORLD THAT WORKS FOR EVERYBODY:

VISIONS OF UTOPIA;

BUCKMINSTER FULLER AND ME

by

Professor
'MARVIN MARVIN' SUROWITZ

Edited, Additions & Cover Art

by

S.J. FLECK

BIOS

MARVIN SUROWITZ
a.k.a. 'MARVIN MARVIN'

Marvin is a professor of Political Science. He has been teaching college since 1964. Students say his class is a pivotal point in their lives.

Since the 1960's Marvin has been involved in social and political issues: environmental, human rights and peace. He has run for political office.

He's travelled to over 35 countries so far.

In the 1970's Marvin studied with R. Buckminster Fuller, the famed architect, writer and futurist. 'Bucky' declared "Humanity could be a success on Spaceship Earth..." through technology and thinking "outside of the box."

"When I was a child there was a TV show called "Queen for a Day" where the "lucky" winner (the one with the most compelling sad story) was awarded most of her heart's desires: a new washer, TV, money, etc. I dreamed of being "King for a Day," where I might right the world's wrongs -- hunger, poverty, discrimination, injustice.

I soon realized I would need more than one day to right these wrongs -- more than one week -- perhaps more than one lifetime. In my best moments I see people as One. I see the Earth working. I see peace and prosperity. I see no wars. I see sustainable and equitable growth. I see Earth Community!" I see God's vision.

'Marvin Marvin' Surowitz is the founder and

Executive Director of Earth Community, Inc.

Marvin is a lifetime Detroit area resident.

Marvin continues teaching Political Science, as he has since 1964.

He is a parent, grandparent, mentor, world traveler, author, community organizer, freedom advocate, and an accomplished public speaker. Most importantly he is a visionary and a peacemaker. Marvin was born into and believes in the Judeo-Christian traditions.

S.J. FLECK

Steven Joseph Fleck holds a Bachelor of Science in Telecommunication and Film, with a Minor in Art Photography, and a Bachelor of Fine Arts in Graphic Design. He is an artist, musician, DJ, political voice and resident of Detroit, Michigan.

TABLE OF CONTENTS

A WORLD THAT
WORKS FOR EVERYBODY:

VISIONS OF UTOPIA;

BUCKMINSTER FULLER AND ME

I have a vision about an Earthwide Utopia, and I would like to share this vision with you. Utopia means Perfect Existence. I believe that Utopia is possible and desirable for both the individual and society.

A Utopia is a perfect place: People are happy; they have enough to eat; their material needs are met; they feel they belong. A Utopia has no war, no pollution, and no alienation. Is Utopia only in imagination and dreams. Can it exist in physical reality? Let us explore the prospects together.

The news today is depressing. We hear about wars, about hunger, about pollution, about the death of different species of animal and plant life. Our oceans are threatened. Mankind itself is in danger of extinction.

In 1971, the National Science Foundation added the species homosapien, otherwise known as humankind, to the list of endangered species.

Humanity joined the hundreds of other mammal, bird, plant, and reptilian species whose life on this planet is in grave jeopardy. In our case it is not a question of our failure to adapt to the changing moods and cycles of nature. We are fouling our own nest.

Also in 1971, Jacques Cousteau, the world's foremost underwater explorer, made a prediction that the death of the world's oceans would take place within the next fifty years. In Washington D.C., for a conference on ocean pollution, Cousteau said that the destruction of the oceans from pollution is already 20 to 30 percent complete. The pollution of the continental shelves within the oceans is our gravest ecological threat. The shelves encompass three percent of the total ocean area and extend only to depths of a few hundred feet – depths; which the rays of the sun can still penetrate. The shelves provide the home for the vast majority of all the photo -synthesis-supported marine plant life. Therefore, the continental shelves actually support most of the life within the ocean.

The problem is that these ocean areas which are so close to the land are where much of our man-made pollution is accumulating. Polluted rivers do not flow into wide open oceans, but tend to accumulate on the continental shelves. The vast oceans are largely desert – incapable of supporting either fish or plant life. Only the continental shelves can support this life. We derive as much as 50 percent of our oxygen supply from the plant life within these small areas. If Jacques Cousteau's predictions are correct, within a very short time humankind will be without its major sources of oxygen as well as major sources of food supply. Yet little is being done to correct this situation. It looks like business as usual pending annihilation.

[The most recent unnatural disaster to hit the world is the surge of oil leaked by British Petroleum (BP), which has leaked over 300 million gallons of crude oil into the Gulf of Mexico. It has created some underwater deposits of oil about 6 miles wide.]

Is this the way it has to be? Must we destroy ourselves and our civilization as well as Earth itself? Can't anything be done?

People all over the Earth, in every country, are basically good. They don't want to see humans become extinct or this planet destroyed. They see us in trouble but they don't know what to do to set things right. They don't know about alternatives.

Alternatives are choices. People can choose to do better if they know Alternatives. This book deals with Alternatives. It gives an outline of a future to aim and plan for. It takes concepts of Ecology and puts them into potential living reality. You may see that Utopia, Perfect Existence, is both possible and within reach.

ORIGINS OF THE WORD - UTOPIA

The word 'Utopia' was first coined by Sir Thomas More when he published his short political fantasy of that name in the year 1516. But the idea which it represents, the perfect state of human happiness and harmony, has existed since the dawn of humankind.

It is interesting to note that the word 'Utopia' was derived from two Greek words, "ou", meaning "no", and "topos" meaning "place". Thus Utopia was "no place" or "no where" in the physical world, at least during Sir Thomas More's time.

But if Utopia is 'no, where' it is also 'now, here'. Utopia was not possible when people thought there was only enough for a very small minority to live in comfort. Today, thanks to increasing knowledge, while most people lived in need and desire for such a place, and increasing technology, the prospects for Utopia are indeed "now here."

FUTURISM

The study of where the future is taking us is called "futurism". People who think, plan, study, teach, and write our future are called "futurists".

Futurists can look at the future in either positive, negative, or objective terms. Aldous Huxley's book '*Brave New World*' and George Orwell's book '*1984*' describe negative future states. The book '*Future Shock*', by Alvin Toffler, describes our future in an objective way, though one notes a continual theme of optimism throughout. In this book we describe positive future alternatives.

BUCKMINSTER FULLER

I would like to introduce you to a most important futurist. His full name is R. Buckminster Fuller. A lot of people drop the "R", and some just call him "Bucky". Bucky calls himself a "long distance thinker". This is because he likes to think in as broad of terms as possible.

{Note: Buckminster Fuller died in 1983 at the age of 87.}

"How big can you think?" Bucky asks. Can you think about the whole Earth and solutions to the Earth's problems? Can you think about the Universe and its relationship to the Earth? That's what Bucky does. Can you make the world work?

Fuller has dedicated his life to making this planet work. He's dedicated to discovering "the principles operating in the Universe". He says these principles need not be invented: They exist already. And as these principles are discovered, we, in turn, discover that it's possible for us to live our lives in harmony on a self-sustaining, self-regenerating Earth.

The intelligence that created our Universe, our 'Cosmos', and our Planet within this framework, created with infinite wisdom and intelligence.

Science and religion are rediscovering this all the time. This intelligence can provide for our needs and allow us to lead our lives in happiness if we tune ourselves to it.

As it is written in the Old Testament: "Prove me now, saith the Lord, and see if I shall not pour thee out blessings and there shall not be room enough for you to receive them"

FULLER COMPARED TO OTHER SOCIAL-ECONOMIC THINKERS

Throughout recorded history, various persons have put forth social-economic premises and have voiced their projections about humanity's future. Let us look at some of these ideas and then compare them with Buckminster Fuller's views.

Malthus: The world's population will multiply more rapidly than the available food supply.

Darwin: Only the fittest will survive.

Marx: The workers who produce things are the fittest because they are the only ones who know how to produce physically and therefore they ought to be the ones to survive.

Fuller: Technology providing more and more goods from fewer and fewer resources can guarantee that all humanity would survive.

He goes on to say,

"It is very logical that man should fight to the death when he thinks there's not enough to go around.

"In a fire, he loses all reason, goes mad, and tramples his fellow men to death as he competes for air.

"It is also very logical that man won't fight when he knows there's enough to go around. It is logical, It is logical. It is logical."

One of Fuller's books is entitled 'Utopia or Oblivion'. In this book he says that we either move to establish Utopia or else we obliterate – destroy – ourselves from this planet.
According to Fuller there really seems to be no middle ground between Utopia and oblivion. If we continue as we have been we will soon destroy ourselves. If we make only a few changes, a few reforms, we will soon again find ourselves close to the brink of destruction. Yes, a perfected society it must be! Utopia is our alternative to oblivion.

In our future society, when we have ended war, made rational use of our natural resources, and utilized technology and computers, then we will see that we will have more than "enough to go around".

Unlike earlier revolutions, in our 'evolutionary Utopia', our goal is not to 'bring down certain peoples. Instead, we seek to bring everyone up to the highest standard of living and ecological balance.

Sounds Utopian, doesn't it? But remember, "Utopia is our alternative to oblivion."

SPACESHIP EARTH

An interesting thing about planet Earth is that it is really a Spaceship!

During each hour our Spaceship travels sixty thousand miles around the Sun and also spins one thousand miles on its own axis. It is thanks to the laws of gravity and physics that we all don't fall off!

Our Spaceship is happily endowed with a Sun and a Moon which are flying in company with us, as well as mineral and fossil fuel deposits which are on board. The Sun is our major energy source. It is traveling with us at just the right distance to keep us alive and allow plant life to grow, yet it is not close enough to burn us up.

The Moon provides our Spaceship with light by night. It also controls the flow of the tides which are another energy source. The Moon also has great effects on our Spaceship's weather.

Aboard our Spaceship are great energy sources, deposited below the surface in the form of mineral stockpiles and vast amounts of fossil fuel deposits.

It is due to the energy radiations from the Sun, the gravitational pulls by the Moon, and the energy within the mineral and fossil fuel stockpiles deposited on Earth, that we can say that we, the Earth's inhabitants, have been given an extremely favorable environment in which to live a full and rich life.

We can observe that, in reality, the Sun, the Moon, and the Earth, are a fantastically well designed team of space programmed vehicles.

Isn't it strange that on this one unique planet; a planet that's getting smaller every day due to the speed of communication and the ease of transportation, that we have artificially divided it up into over 200 separate nations? We have divided our Earth home by boundaries, passports, and border checks; by barbed wire, huge barrier walls and warfare.

If a nation were to launch a spaceship into space and everyone aboard that spaceship spoke different languages and everyone aboard was suspicious of everyone else; chances are that spaceship would never reach its destination.

Such a situation is true of our Spaceship Earth at this time. Nations speak different languages and all the nations are equally suspicious of each other. It would seem that if we continue in this manner our Spaceship is never going to reach its destination but is instead going to crash land.

But what is our Destination? According to Fuller, our Destination is to populate the Universe.

EARTH MEN; EARTH WOMEN; EARTH CHILDREN; EARTH BEINGS;

...ONE EARTH

We people of this Earth Planet have more in common than that which divides us. It used to be that if one group of people lived on one side of a mountain, they would be afraid of those living on the other side. This fear was based on unfamiliarity and lack of knowledge. It was based on superstition. Today we know people on the other side of the mountain and on the other side of the world.

We know that people on Earth share similar life patterns. We are born, and are more or less formally educated, develop relationships with those around us, often settling into a marriage situation, produce and provide for offspring, search for the causes and nature of our existence, grow older and die.

In significant ways, all Earth People are the same. There is no reason to hate anyone. We're all on this planet together!

We are all really Earth People. Riders on Spaceship Earth Together: Earth Women, Earth Men, Earth Children and Earth Beings.

Our Utopia would consist of a single Earth Nation. No boundaries, separate nations, or warring countries. We are not tourists of the

Earth: Earth is our home. As Socrates said, "I am not an Athenian or a Greek, but a citizen of the world." Now, 2400 years later, we could truly establish, in the words of Marshall McLuhan, an Earth "Global Village".

Our one Earth nation would eliminate the competitive need for war. Eliminating war would free the resources, now wasted on war, and allow then to be applied toward peaceful ends.

War is costly. Each year the nations of the earth spend almost two trillion dollars on warfare. They build and test bombs, invent new weapons, and pour manpower and resources into destruction. In earlier times war may have brought honor and nobility to its heroes. The very moment, however, that you realize that war is unnecessary, destructive and ineffective; every bit of honor it confers is gone.

Why is it that countries always make money and resources available to fight wars but the money never seems to be available to do the things needed to correct the imbalances which cause war in the first place, namely, producing enough to go around for everybody Earthwide? Politicians seem to reject peaceful projects, like rebuilding cities or building water treatment facilities, by saying "it costs too much," or that "it can't be done." There is a misconception. Humanity can afford to do anything it needs and wishes to do.

People all over the Earth are beginning to awaken to the fact that this is a beautiful and most perfect planet, and what we call heaven can be right 'Here and Now' on Earth. One group of U.S. astronauts returning from a Moon expedition

reported that on the Moon they had a chance to
see the Earth and the entire Solar System in a
new perspective. Only the Earth was alive. The
other planets were dark, grey, and devoid of life.
The Earth was literally beautiful, gleaming with
blues from the waters and greens from the forests
and a multitude of other colors. Here on Earth,
alone was Life.

One astronaut suggested that every person on Earth
should have the opportunity to view the planet
from this perspective and, in his words, "realize
that we're all really Citizens of the Spaceship
Earth."

We Earth People are beginning to appreciate that
we are all sisters and brothers. We are all of the
same spirit: Just as the word, 'uni-verse'
– 'toward one', implies.

ENERGY:
OUR PLANET AS A SELF-REGENERATING,
SELF-SUSTAINING SYSTEM

Imagine a person living in a wooden house.
Everyday he cuts a little more of his house away
to burn for fuel in his fireplace. You might say
that this person was crazy. He's burning up his
own home. Yet this is exactly that we are doing in
relation to our Earth. Every day we are
cutting up, mining out, or pumping away, parts of
our Earth. We are burning up bits and pieces of
our Earth home for fuel to heat our houses, power
our machines, automobiles and factories.

It is this burning of fossil fuels, in the forms
of coal, gas, and oil, which are the major causes

of our pollution problems.

The production of nuclear power causes thermal pollution (the heating of large amounts of water), produces fallout, and raises the question of disposal of the nuclear wastes.

Certainly the signs of pollution are telling us that we shouldn't be burning up our Earth home.

Moreover, the Earth is running out of much of its supply of fossil fuels. World crude oil may not be available beyond about 2050. After those years, and perhaps even before then, petroleum will have become too valuable as a material necessary to the production of synthetic protein foods, plastics and other products for it to be burned as a fuel.

World supplies of coal as an energy source will last only until sometime in the 22nd century.

Nuclear fuels will be exhausted in about 100 years, but with efficient breeder reactors they could be extended, much longer. If efficient breeders are not developed (and these have strong ecological drawbacks) and large new uranium reserves are not found, worked reserves of uranium are not sufficient to supply just the anticipated U.S. demands through the end of this century.

Buckminster Fuller points out: "Geologists have estimated that it costs about one billion dollars in hours and energy expended - for the development of every gallon of petroleum. But yet there is enough energy in ten minutes of one hurricane to match the nuclear stockpiles of the world."

We see that up until this point we have made
ourselves dependent on non-renewable energy
resources which have finite quantity limits. Our
resources are running out and until that time they
are polluting.

Are there Alternatives? The answer is a
resounding, "Yes, there are many." Let us utilize
the natural forces in nature to gain our required
energy. We can do so quite easily. There appears
to be somewhat of a conspiracy on the part of the
oil, gas, and electrical producers to deny us
information about energy alternatives and
seriously underfund all projects which use our
imagination for providing us with energy in a
nonpolluting, natural way; instead of in a
polluting, ecologically destructive way.

Let us now shed a little light on the subject of
Alternative Energy.

We shall learn that we can harness the power of
the Sun: Solar power; the power of the Moon:
Lunar power; the power of the tides, the winds,
the rains, the heat within the Earth
[Geothermal Power], and the magnetic field
produced by the spinning of the Earth to produce
the necessary energy to power our machines. We
need not destroy the Earth. We need not get rid of
our machines. All is right with the World.

SOLAR POWER

Technologists could, if given the proper material
support, harness the power of the sun to run
almost all of our machines. The energy from the
sun is free. The sun is always there, reliably,

for the next several hundred million years. When the sun is not shining on one side of the Earth it is shining on the other.

This solar power can be collected either by putting space satellites into orbit and transmitting electrical power down to Earth from these, or by setting up receiver centers here on Earth in our large desert areas. From these receiver centers electrical power can be transmitted underground by way of electrical power cable networks from one end of Earth to the other.

According to the National Science Foundation, "If we take the energy that reaches Earth and convert it at maybe 10 percent efficiency, we can produce all of our energy needs with less than three percent of our land area."

Individual buildings are being heated by solar power. One method of accomplishing this would be the following:

The roof of the building is equipped with glass panels. The panels are tilted south toward the sun at a 45 degree angle and contain aluminum plates to capture the sun's heat. The heat warms water piped through the panels. The water then travels through to all of the rooms in the building and is stored in the end in a large storage tank to be reused again. The Romans used Solar Power to heat water over 2000 years ago.

LUNAR AND TIDAL POWER

Have you ever wondered why the Moon has such an

effect on the tidal movement of waters — pulling them one direction in the morning and another direction at night? All ordained by the Universe. This movement of water generates energy. This energy can be harnessed.

One method of harnessing these moving waters is to build underwater turbines used as 'windmills'. These windmills would be turned by the moving waters and thereby capture and generate energy. The windmills would be constructed so that their direction would easily reverse itself with the incoming and outgoing tides.

In addition, these turbine windmills would be used to capture the energy of bodies of water which move in only one direction. For example, waters in the Florida Gulf stream move at speeds up to 5.5 miles an hour. All of this movement can be harnessed.

Provisions must be made for marine life to go through or around the windmills without harm. We would also need assurance that excess heat would not be created by their slow moving generators.

WIND POWER

The power of the winds has already been utilized to move the windmills of the Netherlands. Windmills can also help generate electricity for homes worldwide.

Windmills have been developed which can operate in winds of only 3 to 4 mph and can produce electricity at the rate of 70 kilowatts a minute; enough to meet the power needs of 4 families.

What happens when there is no wind? Well, according to experts, this happens only three days a month in most parts of the world. Moreover, the power generated on windy days can be used to charge storage batteries for use when the wind drops in velocity.

Wind Power, together with Solar Power would allow for a completely self-sufficient home in terms of necessary energy to run all appliances and for heating and cooling purposes.

RAINWATER POWER

We could even harness the energy produced by the tapping pressure of falling rains upon the Earth.

GEOTHERMAL POWER

Geothermal power is the natural heat deposits from the Earth's core. Properly harnessed geothermal energy could provide us with much of our energy needs.

The source of most geothermal energy is molten rock, or magma, lying a few miles beneath the Earth's crust. When underground water comes in contact with the magma, hot steam and water are produced.

When this occurs in large quantities and within a few miles of the Earth's surface, the steam and hot water can be tapped and used to turn turbines that generate electricity.

This electricity can then be used to heat buildings, desalinate sea water and even extract valuable minerals from the steam or hot water that carries the energy.

Although fewer than 15 countries currently are attempting to tap subterranean energy, and so far only on a small scale, at least 80 nations have geological conditions indicating geothermal reservoirs and geothermal potential.

FUSION POWER

Instead of nuclear power plants which burn uranium and present us with the problems of nuclear fallout, disposal of nuclear wastes, thermal pollution, and the frightening human peril in case of accident, we will move toward fusion power.

Fusion power plants draw for fuel on deuterium and tritium, two heavy forms of hydrogen. There is practically an unlimited supply of deuterium in the oceans and tritium is a man-made isotope produced as a by-product of the operation of the fusion plants themselves. At temperatures of millions of degrees these elements fuse together to produce helium atoms, releasing vast amounts of usable energy.

Fusion power does not produce any radioactive byproducts or other pollutants. Heat being dispersed from this fusion process could be safely and economically used to heat buildings or other similar uses. Commercially produced fusion power may be a reality in our future.

METHANE POWER

Methane power is the energy in the form of gas which is released during the decay and fermentation of animal and human excrement, as well as 'garbage', sewage, and vegetable wastes.

Methane fuel can be produced on either a small or large scale. Already individually owned automobiles and trucks have been converted to run off of methane power.

On a large scale, garbage-burning facilities have been established. The process is started with fuel oil and, once burning, garbage is fed into the facility. The gases released are converted into fuel which will both keep the facility operating and produce additional energy.

The hemp plant is a great source for methane.

HYDRO-ELECTRIC POWER

A safe method of producing energy already used extensively, but one which could be used to a greater degree in our future, is Hydro-Electric Power. This is power produced by a body of water naturally flowing in its course and falling off a cliff or rock formation, and continuing its course downstream. The energy of this falling water can be captured. Extensive dams and reservoirs can be built for this purpose, providing they do not cause any ecological problems by their development.

TRANSMISSION OF POWER

An important key to world unity will be our increasing ability to transmit electrical power over longer and longer distances, and to integrate the existing electrical supply systems of many countries and continents. Our existing technology allows us transmission of this electrical energy for 3000 miles via underground transmission cables with a transmission loss no greater than 10 percent. Improved technology would allow us to transmit for even greater distances.

This new integration renders the cost of power relatively cheap, and enables the development of hydroelectricity in any part of the world. Once local needs are met, surplus energy will be available to meet needs elsewhere. This allows demands for power to be shared by several electrical supply systems. The power of the Yukon (where there is little demand) could be transmitted to Los Angeles, if necessary.

As Buckminster Fuller points out, this new ability to transport electrical energy over long distances means an integration of the electrical producing capacities of such countries as the U.S.A. with Russia and even the People's Republic of China, thereby providing reserve power for each. This will likely translate into tremendous economic gain for the countries involved, for the Earth as a whole, as well as for the causes of peace.

INTEGRATED HOUSEHOLD ENERGY AND RECYCLING SYSTEMS

In our Utopian society all homes would have their

own integrated water systems which would replace the need for a piped in water supply and outside sewer systems. Rain basins would collect and store water for future use on lawns and gardens. This water could also be used in the home after the water has been filtered and purified.

Homes would be equipped with a biological waste treatment unit which would treat sewage and waste with a bacteria treatment and then either transport the treated waters to an outside compost pile, for use in a landscape irrigation system, or for the production of methane power for the home.

The water closets in the toilets would be redesigned for a 'dry' flush, instead of the current average 2.5 to 5 gallons used each time the toilet is flushed.

Refuse, i.e., paper, old tools, old clothes, etc., would be picked up weekly and recycled by the appropriate agencies within the society.

Homes would also be equipped to generate their own electrical, heating and cooling systems by means of wind power and solar panels. Homes would be well insulated against the cold and would also be nestled among the trees so as to protect them from the hottest rays of the sun.

DOWN COME THE POWER LINES AND THE MONTHLY BILLS FROM THE UTILITY COMPANIES.

ENERGY: PARTING COMMENTS

What we then find is that this planet Earth is a

self-sustaining and self-regenerating system. We discover that it is no longer necessary to burn up our planet for energy sources and create pollution in the process.

Bucky says that the fossil fuels were part of a big safety factor on Spaceship Earth which allowed humankind to be ignorant for a long time until we had really learned how to run our Spaceship. The fossil fuels were meant as 'starter fuels'. Now we have the insight and the capacity to 'run' off of the main 'engine' and our primary energy sources — the sun, moon, winds, and water. Fuller compares the Sun and the moon to the generator and alternator of an engine: together they constitute the prime generator and alternator of our life support system.

In reality, the Sun, Moon, and Earth are nothing less than a fantastically well designed team of space vehicles. Bringing the Sun, Wind, and Earth back into technology, represents a revolutionary renewal of our tie to nature.

Bucky writes:

"Just as a baby chick breaks through the shell of its egg when its food supply inside the egg has been exhausted, so we find ourselves just about to step out from our one—second-ago broken eggshell. Our innocent trial-and-error sustaining nutriment is exhausted. We are faced with an entirely new relationship to the universe. We are going to spread our wings of intellect and fly or perish."

A CHAPTER ON TECHNOLOGY

TECHNOLOGY

Our proposed Utopia is possible today because of technology. Technology is the science and study of the practical or industrial arts.

We now have the Technology: the knowledge, the automated factories, and the computers, to be able to produce enough to satisfy all of the world's material needs.

Some people have suggested that the only way we can survive on this planet is to immediately rid ourselves of almost all of technology. They want us to go back to what they see as a more ideal time before machinery was introduced on such a large scale. Most people, however, do not want to give up our technological progress.

Buckminster Fuller says that not only can we keep our technology but that our technology is what, in fact, will save us. What we must create is an overview in relation to Technology. We can keep, and continually develop, our technology. Only, let us utilize the best technology possible.

According to Fuller, many people live today under an illusion that "there's not enough to go around". These people fight and compete over who is going to get 'what' from 'whom'. They falsely believe that there is a 'scarcity' of items.

While the myth that "there is not enough to go around" may have been true in the past, Bucky insists that it certainly isn't true of our future. Even today our machinery, our technology, is capable of producing so much that everyone Earthwide can get enough of what they want and what they need. We, as an Earth society, can move "beyond scarcity".

Before technology, one person out of 100 lived in some degree of wealth, supported by the labor of a struggling 99%. No machinery had been developed to free humanity from the burden of hard manual labor. Thus, that 99% often lived short and brutal lives of "quiet desperation" —an inequality which still exists in many parts of the world today that have not yet entered into the Technological Age.

Today, thanks to technology, we all have the potential, Earthwide, to live lives of material abundance. Technology is turning out to be the great Liberator of the Earth's peoples.

AUTOMATION AND CYBERNETICS

Our factories can be, and are being, fully automated so that human labor is reduced to a minimum and the machines do almost all of the work. After all, that's what the machines were designed for in the first place.

Given the benefits that automation offers, we should not seek to limit its usefulness. A man or woman working with their muscles is capable of producing at 1/20 of a horsepower per hour. In contrast, one kilowatt hour of electricity is equal to 26 man-hours. Amarica's capacity to convert electrical energy, as opposed to muscle power is over 38 billion kilowatt hours per week. The total horsepower capacity of all Earth's people

working with their muscles is very small.
Therefore it makes sense to use machine power and
automation to produce the goods humanity needs.
Of course, the sources of this electrical power
should be from non-polluting, ecological sources.
Human hours of labor have become much less
significant in the face of the greatly advanced
technological development which has taken place
over the last 100 years or so.

Even the supervision of the automated machines and
the inspection of the goods produced by these
machines can be done by advanced self-regulating
computers. This Science of Computers is called
Cybernetics. Many people suggest that we have
entered into a Cybernetic Age.

DESIGN SCIENCE

At a much earlier point in time, inventors often
made fortunate discoveries quite by accident.
Today you can explain to engineers your
problem or project and they will be able to design
and construct the necessary machinery to carry out
your plan.

Do you want to design a spacecraft that can carry
many people to distant planets? Just give the
scientists and technologists the necessary
resources and they will likely be able to design
this spacecraft. This new science of 'design' is
aptly called "design science".

Design science can also increase the efficiency of
our materials and the fuel consumption:
production ratios meaning that less fuel would be
needed to produce more goods. Design science can

increase the efficiency in design of our machines and the structures that house them, as well as those structures that house 'humankind'.

MORE WITH LESS

We are also learning how to produce more efficiently with fewer materials. "More with less", this is called. The first telephone wires carried a single massage; today they carry billions. Computers and satellites are becoming more compact even as their work loads increase. The best air conditioners work more efficiently with less power. Every discovery leads to further discovery and teaches us how to do more with less. Technology is moving toward the miniature.

INCREASING THE EFFICIENCY OF OUR MATERIALS, OUR FUEL CONSUMPTION, AND OUR PHYSICAL MACHINERY

According to Buckminster Fuller, the vast majority of today's machinery is operating at an appallingly low overall mechanical-efficiency level at which the machines realize, in terms of energy work done, only 1/25th, or 4% of the potential of the energy they consume. In the area of housing, the figure is even worse. In this area we presently realize that less than 1% overall structural efficiency in respect to the now known capabilities of materials used in building, i.e. "we could build one hundred comparably volumed and useful buildings out of the same weight, time, and energy-resources units now ignorantly processed into one building." But to advance performance both of energy and of material efficiency involves "comprehensive building and system reorganization".

The energies of automobiles today are running at 5% overall efficiency. The new gas turbines are 30% efficient. Coal-burning turbo-electric generators are 40% efficient. Jet engines are 60% efficient. Combined desalination and electric-power -generating atomic reactors are 72% efficient.

Fuller says that it is feasible by design to triple the present 4% average mechanical-fuel -efficiency to just 12% and "thus take care handsomely of 100% of humanity." The problem is primarily one of upgrading performance by scientific and technological inventions.

It will be through design science—designing new technology, new physical inventions, better efficiency from fuel consumption, and more efficient usage of our Earth material wealth that all humanity will move to prosperity.

Fuller says that in 1900 less than 1% of our world population was enjoying the benefits derived from technological advances. Today this figure has increased to 44%. The continually accelerating rate of increase in the number of people being served with ever higher standards of industrialization has occurred despite the rapid increase in world population and despite the ever-decreasing supply of world metals on a per capita or individual basis. The reason for this increase is our growing ability to continually do more with less per given unit of resources for each function.

Says Fuller: "We must (continually) redesign the

use of the world's total resources in such a manner as to make those now exclusively in the service of only 44% of humanity adequate to the effective service of 100% of humanity at higher standards of living despite a continually decreasing inventory of those resources."

According to Fuller, this upsurge in our living standards can come about 20 years faster by a deliberate design-science revolution, then it will by waiting for what Fuller says is the unintentional second-hand fallout 20 years later, into the civilian sector of the society technology which was originally developed for warfare. He suggests that "the 20-year-difference could be the difference between humanity's success or extinction."

A TECHNOLOGICAL SYSTEM

Thanks to automation, cybernetics, and "design science", mankind is going to be increasingly freed from the struggle of having to "earn a living". While the machines produce, you and I would be freed from the drudgery and boredom of factory life. Production of goods would no longer be impeded by human beings trying to do what machines can do better. Even now, we are in the process of creating a worldwide super-industrial society.

Technology properly applied will produce total economic success for humanity and will eliminate the fundamental causes of war, i.e., "you or me to the death - on behalf of yours and mine - for there is not enough for both of us." Technology would show that both Malthus - with his idea that population growth will outrace our capacity to provide food for all of us - and Darwin's idea of survival of only the fittest, were just "pseudo"-scientific notions that we once accepted before realizing that, in fact, we can provide for all.

TECHNOLOGY HELD BACK

Often in today's society, the latest technological discoveries are not utilized because of some peoples' vested interests in keeping things the way that they are. An example of this is the automobile industry's opposition to rapid and mass transit.

The auto interests use their influence in the political and economic world to block mass transit. Unfortunately, like many other people they are still under the illusion that "there's not enough to go around."

The auto interests are fighting and competing to keep the privileges which they have in this 'money-scarcity' oriented society. They think there is only limited wealth on this planet. They feel they can't share their 'market' with mass transit. The auto interests would rather sell and service autos and build and service roads than assist in developing mass transit.

Sometimes industrialists will purchase patents and simply 'shelf' them to get then out of the way. Often these patents represent great forward gains in innovative research.

It has become common on the American industrial

scene for a company intent on limiting opportunities for its competition, or anxious to avoid the expenditures of money and energy involved in revising its own production techniques, to buy up patents and then lock them up.

The process is even easier if the advance is the 'brain child' of one of that company's employees. Such a person may get a pat on the back and a salary raise while the company sees that the idea never gets into production.

In our future society, what we must do is to see that while inventors and innovators are well rewarded for their discoveries, that their ideas do not remain the private domain of anyone but are shared and utilized by the society as a whole. Private, exclusive domain, patents would no longer be issued.

WILL TECHNOLOGY SPELL OUR DOOM?

As we have learned thus far, the sane uses of technology could transform the world. But technology could also destroy us. If far -reaching plans are not acted on and initiated soon the continued misuse of technology may certainly destroy us. Uncoordinated, uncontrolled technology can forecast our Doom.

But again, technology need not do this. If we encourage our scientists, engineers, and technicians to make use of the most moral aspects of their beings, and, in turn, free them from the machinations of political power, and economic motivations and allow them to function with the impartial but precise computations and revelations of the computer – then we will well be on our way to our Technological Liberation.

Moreover, we must inform and educate the general population so that they will understand the workings and the consequences of the technological superstructure. This will be a great protection against the misuse of technology by anyone or anything.

In conclusion, it is clear that technology must be judged by the consequences of its uses. Harmful and destructive technological consequences must be avoided. Technological feasibility does not necessarily imply social or cultural feasibility. Technology without understanding and planning overview is a frightening prospect. We must educate and organize ourselves so that this will not continue to happen.

SPACE RESEARCH, ITS CONTRIBUTIONS TO OUR UTOPIAN TECHNOLOGY

Our proven ability to transport ourselves into outer space, to the Moon, and to other planets may very well be the key to our survival on Earth also. Thanks to space research we are learning many things about how to keep humans alive while they are far from the life-sustaining conditions unique to Planet Earth.

As Fuller suggests, as we plan on sending Earth people on a prolonged trip through space we had better design the equipment -- the life -sustaining equipment -- to keep them alive throughout the trip. These discoveries and inventions which are made for space travel have application for life here on Earth also. After all, if we can design the technology to send Earth Beings to the Moon and back, we certainly can design the technology to make Earth Beings a success on this Home Planet.

Some spin-offs of the U.S. space program are: laser surgery, nuclear-powered human heart aids, dialysis machines for artificial kidneys, air-transportable hospitals and pharmacy, computerized cargo, and portable total energy packages.

Just as we go off to a new planet in a spacecraft which we know isn't going to get any new equipment, we are discovering that we ourselves are aboard a space vehicle that is not going to get any new equipment, which yet could be operated as a success for all.

In our Utopia Space Research would be encouraged and we may indeed find ourselves able to travel and support life anywhere in the Universe, especially here on our home planet.

'CONTRIBUTIONS' OF WAR TO OUR TECHNOLOGY AND OUR HIGHER LIVING STANDARDS

Incredible as it may seem at first glance, war has actually brought us many benefits in a technological sense as well as so much brutality and destruction. Technology that was developed for warfare has been converted into technology for peaceful consumption after the war had reached its conclusion.

These adaptations developed when the contractors who had produced the advanced technology for war found themselves, in the words of Fuller, "'all dressed up,' with the tools, the scientists, and the skilled workers, and no 'defense' contracts. The home market then became an unexpected bonanza."

Examples of the technological innovations that were developed because of warfare, but found their way into the consumer market are electric generators, steam boilers, electric lights, radio, oil burners, refrigerators, and air conditioners. All were developed for battleships, for example.

[More recently, one of the most recent inventions made for military use that has come to the mass public are GPS devices. You can even find them installed on most cell phones. Portable phones can be seen as a device that was also originally thought of a military device.]
Fuller states that:

"Those who suggest that it might all have developed peacefully are as unrealistic as are those who now think that the old patterns can continue without man annihilating man."

A RECYCLABLE TECHNOLOGY:
PLANETARY SYSTEMS MANAGEMENT

In our future society we will work to develop a fully recyclable technology. We cannot afford nor allow the waste of our valuable resources. We will trace every material of an artifact back to its origin in a natural cycle and forward it again to its re-absorption in a cycle.

Products will be durable: they will be engineered to last.

Excess packaging: three wrappers for one piece of gum will disappear.

Bottles will be returnable and refillable. We will make bottles from biodegradable plastic instead of glass so as to cut down on breakage.

[Most soda manufacturers have already switched over to plastic or aluminum because of the price of glass. Also, many other manufacturers of liquid beverages have switched to plastic or lined cardboard containers.]

NOTES ON GLASS BOTTLES VS. RETURNABLES

The nation's small bottlers have had a hard time for the past 20 years. In 1957 there were 5200 bottling companies while in 1970 there were less than 2300. There has been a corresponding decline in returnable bottles, since the large bottlers have the financial resources to invest in modern high-speed one-way bottle machines.

The State of Oregon was the first state to ban non-returnable bottles in 1973. According to Rich Chambers, an environmentalist who has been publicizing the law, it has been a "great success." [Continued on Pg. 35]

NO GARBAGE -- NO POLLUTION

In our Utopia, nothing will be discarded until it has been inventoried and examined for its salvageable qualities. These will be salvaged and recycled.

Newspapers and magazines will be recycled. All paper wrapping, cardboard, etc., will be recycled.

Leftover food, otherwise known as 'garbage', will be returned to the ground in the form of compost heaps. People may realize that the word 'garbage' is only a myth.

Fuller suggests that there is no such thing as pollution. Those things we falsely consider 'pollution' are the chemical byproducts of industrial processes which could be recaptured and recycled into, once again, productive forms. Rather than allowing these chemicals to be spewed from industrial smokestacks, only to be retrieved from human lungs. We could economize and clean up the environment, by capturing them as part of the original industrial process.

We will accumulate data on mankind's renewable and non-renewable resources. We will work diligently to salvage the world's precious metals lying in 'junk' yards and in ships at the bottom of the oceans. We will develop sound 'planetary systems engineering' with a planetary data bank. The data stored in this bank, similar to Fuller's "World Game", will provide the basis for 'planetary systems management.' The Earth will be viewed as a whole entity.

Through planetary systems management we will be able to examine the ravages caused by the earlier unchecked industrial growth. We will seek to rectify these ravages wherever possible.

We will develop ways to best utilize our earth's mineral and natural resources, using efficiently only what we need. As we need it.

RETURNABLE BOTTLES: CONTINUED

I find it incredible that any responsible government would continue to allow non-returnable bottles and disposable cans. These bottles and cans litter the countryside and endanger a person's ability to walk barefoot. They are simply a convenience for the pop and beer bottlers, not for anyone else in society. The bottlers save a great deal of money by not having to pick up, clean, and re-use their bottles. The pop and beer drinking segments of our society must pay the actual costs of the one-way bottles and cans and society as a whole must pay for their clean-up.

It is estimated that is costs government more than $1.00 to pick up and dispose of each carelessly littered bottle or can. Yet only in the states of Michigan, Oregon, and in a few scattered municipalities have people moved to ban these non-returnables.

It is sad that the beautiful sand dunes around the Great Lakes are disappearing: the sand is being carted off to be converted into glass bottles and the general public is denied access to the scenic beauty on the land surrounding these bodies of water as the big bottling companies buy this land in order to steal its sand.

In our future society; access to land surrounding bodies of water would be open and free and the beaches and recreation areas would go on for miles.

CLEANING UP WATER POLLUTION

Basically our problems of water pollution come from four sources: 1.) Household waste, 2.) Storm runoff, 3.) Industrial wastes, and 4.) Farm and irrigation effluence. The solutions to these problems, however, are not complex.

Household wastes were discussed under "Integrated Household Energy Systems." Briefly: Each home or housing unit would treat and recycle its own wastes.

The second, storm runoff, particularly in cities and other developed areas, would be handled by adequate sewer systems which would convey the water to treatment centers whose function would primarily be the removal of miscellaneous organic matter. The water could then be safely conveyed into rivers and streams, or be delivered directly, again by sewer systems, to various industries for industrial use.

Industrial wastes, the third source, have been a major problem. This would be no longer the case in our future society. The industrial wastewater could be processed right at the plant for the removal of chemical content. The chemicals could then be recycled or reused in the industrial process. In the event that a factory does not have or cannot build this filtering unit, the wastes would be conveyed by a sewer system, separate from the storm sewer systems, to special large water treatment plants where the water could be adequately treated and chemical pollutants removed, hopefully to be reused in the industrial process.

The fourth aspect of our water pollution problems involves farm and irrigation effluence. Often the owners of large animal feed lots simply shovel the animal manure into nearby rivers or streems. This tremendous load often poisons these waterways. The answers to these problems could be quite simple: 1.) We as Earth people might be consuming fewer meat products, therefore fewer animals will produce less effluence. 2.) Our society would be cutting down on the use of chemical fertilizers, thereby creating a 'market' for manure fertilizers. 3.) We would also be using manure for methane fuel production.

Finally, incredible as it might seem, cow manure can be cleaned and processed into high protein feed for animals.

TRANSPORTATION

Transportation is a vital consideration both today and in our future society. We enjoy our mobility: we like our environment and we like to travel to discover the range and variety of our Earth neighbors. But we need to consider that transportation is our greatest consumer of energy. And most of this energy, particularly when it comes to the individually owned car, is wasted.

The individually owned car has had a great liberating effect in every society where cars have been introduced on a mass scale. Thanks to the automobile, people have been able to explore their world. They have been freer from society's restraints. But, perhaps, the time has come: Practical and ecological considerations indicate that the era of the individually owned cars might have to be reconsidered.

Cars pollute: 60% of the air pollution in cities is caused by automobiles. Cars kill: 50,000 auto deaths in the United States alone, and over 250,000 injuries. Cars take up much space: More than half the actual space in cities is devoted to the care, feeding, driving, and parking space of automobiles.

Every year more and more open space is destroyed and more and more urban areas are altered in order to make additional room for highways. This is true, not only in the United States but in the entire world. Cars are important status symbols to most people and so to suggest alternatives to the automobile indicates that they had better be good ones. Among the better alternatives would be rapid transit: Fast moving, efficient, and clean trains, subways, cable cars, and monorails could speed propel from one location to another at speeds up to 100 – 150 miles per hour.

Rapid transit stops within cities would be every several blocks. This rapid transit could be supplemented by a quiet and clean running bus service, which would literally pick up and drop people off at their own doorsteps.

This public transportation would be free, 'paid for' by society-at-large. No-fare transport would free drivers or conductors from concern about fare collection and so enable them to concentrate on driving and service to their passengers. No-fare collection would also simplify much of the bookkeeping involved in providing public transportation.

Most of the rapid transit would not have drivers anyway, but, rather, be run by automated, cybernated equipment.

Increasing numbers of people would take to this free efficient rapid transit and would abandon their automobiles. People would not have their cars taken from them, but would voluntarily limit their use when they see just how much more efficient and safer the mass transit can be.

People could still maintain their cars if they so choose. But they would find their own cars increasingly expensive, especially in comparison to free, fast moving rapid transit.

As the streets become clearer of air pollution and safer because of less auto traffic, more people would choose to enjoy bicycle riding and walking outdoors. Pedestrians could relax and enjoy their streets. Outside cafes would flourish, as would new parks.

Bicycle routes would be established and could be covered by tents whose flaps could be raised or lowered. When it rains the flaps of the tents would immediately be lowered so that the people can continue to use their bicycles on dry paths, and stay dry themselves. The flaps would be raised again when the sun reappears.

Transportation between cities would be by free high-speed trains. Airplane transport over long distances and continents would be available and distributed through the use of Energy Unit Certificates (discussed later under Economics of Our Utopia).

A consideration: the auto factory workers and auto salespersons who would be giving up their auto-related jobs as our Utopia developed would receive new, more secure, shorter hour jobs working with our automated technology or working in service jobs, the arts, or farming. They, therefore, should not fear the displacement of their auto-related jobs by mass transit.

AUTOS / CABLE CARS

The automobiles our society would continue to have would be powered by alternative energy sources such as methane, solar power, or steam. The weight of the automobile would be radically reduced by the use of lightweight metals (or perhaps even rubber). Even then, individually operated automobiles would more than likely be replaced by computerized, fully automatic, personal cable cars.

Each cable car would be a very light capsule, carrying between one and eight passengers. These small vehicles would be run on a lightweight viaduct above the road. These vehicles would play a particularly important transportation role in the very center of cities.

The motor would be electric, perhaps solar powered, and therefore pollution free. The current would flow from the single track.

The cable cars would operate in this manner: An individual, before boarding the vehicle, would go to a ticket agent and tell the agent where he wished to go. The agent, with the aid of computers, would issue a 'programmed' ticket. The individual would walk or be elevated up to the platform, where a vehicle would be waiting, having been summoned by the computer. The vehicle would be a small box-like structure with a large side opening and two pairs of seats facing each other. When the doors are shut, the traveler would insert the ticket into a slot, thereby programming the vehicle to where it should go.

Meanwhile a stream of other vehicles would be flowing along the main track past the station. The central computer which controls all operations would receive information from detectors in the track and would spot a suitable gap in the flow. The vehicle would be commanded to leave the station siding for the main stream. It would then safely and rapidly, perhaps at speeds in excess of 100 m.p.h., carry the individual to the programmed destination.

[For the time being I believe that car companies should focus more on electric cars and other forms of electric transportation. Living in Detroit, it would be of great use if we had a subway system that went out from the city to the suburban areas of Metro Detroit. Especially in the economic climate that Michigan is in, this would increase jobs, and allow for transportation other than

automobiles, and provide much less pollution. Some people that were against electric power are now changing their minds, since it is no way as dirty as fossil fuels, at least in cities]

TRAINS

Trains would be designed of light alloys which would be about half the weight of their counterparts today. Hydraulically-operated body-tilting would enable the trains to round curves at a maximum speed; hydro-dynamic brakes would enable the train to stop in short distances.

Most of the trains would be enclosed in tunnels or in a plastic tube so as to free themselves from weather conditions.

Many trains would shed their wheels and instead ride on a cushion of air. These 'aerotrains' have distinct advantages over ordinary trains. The first is speed. One French Train can go as fast as 225 miles per hour. A second advantage would be the smooth ride provided by the aerotrain.

The aerotrains are supported on a cushion of air, and because they need no wheels and suspension systems – usually the heaviest parts of a train – the concrete rail upon which they are suspended can be very light and therefore cheap. The rail can be elevated so that the train runs above a road or conventional railway, thereby minimizing land costs.

One of the problems of air cushion trains is estimating their power cost. Energy is needed to lift the vehicle off the ground as well as to push it forward. Answers to these problems are being explored by technologists today.

[High speed trains are our current future. As of right now, the U.S. is planning on and working on high speed rail lines to cross the country, much like the ones already existing in Japan. And really, it would not be that much more to travel the globe on these lines. Eventually we will be using magnetic / electro-magnetic technology to travel across the world. We must begin to conserve Helium, which is a key component in magnets, in order to make this a real possibility, since Helium is starting to run out.]

AIRPLANES

Today the great misery of traveling by airline is the time it takes to get from the city center out to the airport. One part of the answer is to be found in rapid transit connecting all parts of the city with the airports. The other part is in the use of 'vertical takeoff aircraft' operating from airports within the city centers themselves.

The port for a vertical takeoff airplane would be a small fraction of the size of the conventional airport. The aircraft would rise to 1000 feet in the air before moving forward and it would make only a small amount of sound compared with the huge wave of noise made by a conventional airplane as it gained altitude. Vertiports could be located right in the city centers.

An aircraft innovation which may come about much

sooner than vertical takeoff airplanes, is the short takeoff aircraft. Short takeoff aircraft would curb the growing land hunger of conventional airports and reduce the area of noise disturbance.

CANAL TRAFFIC

Waterways would link all land areas into systems for moving waterborne freight. All continents could be crisscrossed by a network of inland waterways comprising major rivers and canals linking them. Cargos could be moved along miles of river-canal lifelines as waterborne traffic is actually the cheapest way of moving freight. Technocracy (discussed later), according to its Continental Hydrology Plan, estimates that bulk freight transport could be moved by this system at a cost of approximately 1/11th of a cent per ton mile.

TRANSPORTATION CONCLUDED

One might even consider it cruel and irresponsible to give an individual responsibility over an auto: The auto can be a lethal weapon. As Alvin L. Spivak writes in his incredibly interesting (though somewhat male chauvinist) book exposing the auto from a broad sociological perspective,

'The Immoral Machine',
Milieu Information Services, 1972 –
33 East San Fernando St., San Jose, CA 95113

"The auto is just too complex and worrisome a machine to foist upon every man and woman, people who have enough troubles without it and the lube-jobs, oil changes, oil filter renewals, tune-ups, tire rotations, etc., that autos require a as a matter of routine. All of this is in addition to the non-routine - the blown tire, the broken speedometer cable, the non-latchable door latch, the cracked windshield glass, the stopped-up windshield washer, and the dent you got in the parking lot last week."

Some rapid transit concepts being presented today rely very heavily on the automobile. They propose overhead expressways or automated roadways where you would still drive your car and then either drive or be conveyed from one point to another - usually from the suburbs to the city center and vice versa. But what good are such systems? They are not really a total answer.

In the case where you drive your car yourself there would still be fumes and the danger of accidents, as well as the aggressive cold, metallic attitudes the automobile creates within the individual drivers. In the case where your car is driven on a conveyor belt, there is still the problem of parking it upon arrival at point of destination as well as the pollution, fumes, involved in driving the car to and from the con-veyor belt.

Such transit systems are just attempts by the automobile companies and their subservient officials to keep us chained to an obviously outmoded form of transportation. If so much money is to be spent why can't it be on authentic mass transit which would free us from reliance on the auto?

[Much of what the automobile industry has done

over the years has been linked to the oil industry. They want their money now. They want billions in revenue, while destroying the planet in their wake. They have bought up electric car technology to rid the world of the electric car, which had no problems, barely broke down, and they destroyed all of the cars to get rid of the evidence. It is just now, that the car companies of the U.S. have decided to compete in the world market after failing and going bankrupt. It wasn't since the 80's that car emissions for the Big 3 had changed. But now that they almost disappeared completely they have decided to change their ways. But honestly, they are still controlled by the oil companies and will still be way off from really being able to provide a truly environmentally friendly vehicle.]

A CHAPTER ON THE ECONOMICS
OF OUR UTOPIAN SOCIETY

MONEY?   COMPETITION?

Today, money rules most peoples' lives. Many will do almost anything to acquire it. They believe they have no other alternative. They believe "there is not enough to go around." Many factories will even pour untreated wastes into the waterways because they believe they "can't afford" to do otherwise.

Some people, like farm laborers, fastfood workers, and domestic workers, work very hard all day for little money. Some other people work very little for much money. Even in the so-called 'communist' countries, like China, inequality prevails.

Indeed, most people feel that they are in competition with one another. They feel they are in competition for prestige, jobs, and economic goods.

People want to become 'wealthy'. But what is wealth, anyway? What pleasure can one really gain in today's society even with great material wealth when the society itself is in danger of ecological collapse? What is the sense of being 'rich' in a polluted, dying world?

Once, as I was driving down a main street traffic was stopped and rerouted by police. Road space was needed to make room for the largest yacht I had ever seen. It was being towed to one of the area's many polluted lakes. I wondered what real pleasure the yacht owner would obtain by riding over the ugly waters. They would be riding over industrial wastes and human excrement. Lake Erie actually caught fire from all the combustible waste lying within it.

If this is wealth, then why is it so mismanaged?

Though the necessity for money appears to run our lives, money seems to be a false commodity. During the depression, American workers actually went hungry, while American farmers dumped their milk into rivers and burned their crops. The workers were hungry – and the farmers had the food. The only problem was that the workers had no money – no little pieces of paper – to send to the farmers.

When the people of Michigan need food during the winter months, food is shipped up from Florida, Georgia, California, etc. There is no problem with this system. It all seems quite logical. No one thinks it to be disgraceful, that Michigan can't meet its own food needs during the winter months. Why is there a problem, then, in shipping 'American' food to India or other parts of the Earth when these areas find it temporarily difficult to provide their own food needs? Why should lack of a false commodity like money stop hungry people from being fed?

The Bible clearly says, "Thou shalt have no other gods before Me." Yet so many people have made money – Moloch – into a god more dear to them than rational living with their Earth Sisters and Brothers.

REAL WEALTH IN OUR UTOPIA

Our Earth Society will come to realize that any expenditure of material 'wealth' in order to make our world more functional and beautiful is something it can easily "afford to do" - and would gladly do it.

Buckminster Fuller suggests that:

Our society could measure wealth, not in terms of money in the bank nor on a currency based on gold hoarded in vaults. Wealth would be measured by the amounts of energy, both physical and mental, that are available to solve the problem of making the world work for its present inhabitants and for its future generations. This is wealth -- The physical and mental energy that is available to give us the best life possible.

Fuller Writes:

"Real wealth is indestructible and without practical limit. It can be neither created nor lost - and it leaves one system only to join another - the Law of Conservation of Energy. Real wealth is not gold. Real wealth is knowing what to do with energy."

CONSUMER GOODS IN OUR UTOPIA

How do we propose that our Utopia provide the consumer goods needed in our Society?

First, our Utopia, through automated technology, would produce an abundance of consumer goods, things like clothes, refrigerators, air conditioners, etc. This production would attempt to meet peoples' actual needs – in sharp contrast to today's big business and advertising attempts to manipulate peoples' actions and choices.

Second, these goods would be durable – they would last a very long time. Washing machines, for example, would not be constructed to fall apart after three or four years, but would be made to last indefinitely. They would be constructed so that they could be easily repaired when necessary. A high standard of production excellence would replace the strictly competitive criteria that prevail today.

Thirdly, many things would be provided free of charge to the individual. They would instead be paid for by society as a whole. These things would be rapid transit, medical care, schools, colleges, and vast networks of recreation and community centers.

Television would be free of advertisement, and geared to real interests and education, as well as entertainment. Streets would also be free of billboards and flashing neon lights.

DISTRIBUTION OF CONSUMER FOODS IN OUR UTOPIAN SOCIETY

ENERGY UNIT CERTIFICATES

How would consumer goods be distributed? We could consider this practical, equitable system – For the Earth as a whole we would decide just how much consumer goods we should produce for the year ahead. We would measure, in terms of kilowatt or horsepower hours, how much electrical energy the Earth is capable of converting each year, on a strict non-polluting basis from renewable sources, such as solar or wind power, etc. From this total we would deduct the amount of energy that is necessary to keep the Earth-industrial machine running and providing for a high degree of public services. The remainder of the energy would be converted into production of products for individuals.

Each consumer product would have a price according to how much electrical energy and basic materials went into producing it. A television, for example, might cost 100 energy units. A new shirt might cost 2 energy units.

Energy Unit Certificates distributed around the world would be equal to the total of the goods produced each year. Everyone would be given a 'credit card' and whenever they bought anything, the cost in energy units would be subtracted from their account.

In addition, we would maintain a high speed feedback continuous accounting system which would coordinate operations so as to supply things to people as they are needed. When goods are kept accounted for through the use of Energy Certificates, these transactions would be automatically recorded, computed, and relayed back to the factories.

Money would be replaced by energy unit certificates. People could visit one of the easily accessible distribution centers to select the items they desired.

WORK

Equality of income in terms of consumer goods would mean people would have no reason to continue to chase after money and do anything in the process of trying to accumulate it. There would be no exploitation of the environment, no market hustle, and no robbery. Money would cease to run our lives.

But equality of income would not mean that we would all be the same. Rather, not having to worry about 'earning a living' or about being unemployed. It would free us and allow us to pursue our highest natures. We would have time for doing the things we really want to do: traveling, studying the arts and sciences, meditating, lovemaking, developing ourselves on a personal level, etc.

We would work, yes: But only limited hours. According to a plan devised by a farseeing organization known as a Technocracy

Technocracy, INC.
2475 Harksell Rd.
Ferndale, WA 98248

www.technocracy.org

Each person between the ages of 25 and 45 would work four hours a day, four days a week, twenty weeks of the year. This would be a total of only 320 hours per year. We would be farmers or inventors, artists or distributors of the Society's material goods. The years and the times that we would not be working would be our own.

I feel that the Technocratic model would work out quite well in our Utopia. Let the machines do the work. Let us supervise the work of the machines. But let us work only 16 hours per week.

Eventually the need for workers and work may disappear altogether as our Society stabilizes at a high (but as yet undetermined) living standard. As peoples' material wants are satisfied, if not satisfied, the cybernated, automated factories would be able to cut back in production, thereby further preserving our Earth supply of natural resources. Our society might then enter a kind of 'no growth' state talked about by many ecologists and economists today and written about by philosopher and economist John Stuart Mill in his 'Principles of Political Economy' over a hundred and fifty years ago:

"It is scarcely necessary to remark that a stationary condition of capital and population implies no stationary age of human development. There would be as much scope as ever for all kinds of mental culture, and moral and social progress; as much more likelihood of its being improved when minds cease to be engrossed by the art of getting on. Even the industrial arts might be as earnestly and as successfully cultivated, with this sole difference, that instead of serving no purpose but the increase of wealth, industrial improvements would produce their legitimate effect, that of abridging labor."

THE RICH AND THE POOR

Even the so-called wealthy of today's society would be benefitted by our Utopia. No one would take anything away from them. Rather, through technology, peace, and the sane use of the Earth's resources, we would raise everyone up to a high living standard. No one would be pulled down; everyone would be brought up.

Within our Utopia, property rights would become much less important because of rising general affluence. Possessions would no longer stand between us and a true, clearer, liberated way of seeing the world. Why quarrel over a few paltry material objects when the whole Earth could be yours? People would seek a personal fulfillment instead of material possessions. The economics of scarcity would give way to the economics of Abundance.

Everyone would benefit from the stability and safety that would be available to all. No one would have to worry about thievery or murder or be apprehensive about their children's, their grandchildren's, or even their great grandchildren's futures as they are today when even the very survival of our Spaceship is in question. As Edward Bellamy wrote in his famous novel 'Looking Backward 2000 - 1889', which described the differences between 1889, when the book was written, and a fictional account of a

Utopian Community of the year 2000:

"For thirty years I have lived among them, and yet
I seemed to have never noted before how drawn and
anxious were their faces, of the rich as of the
poor, the refined, acute faces of the educated as
well as the full masks of the ignorant. And well
it might be so, for I saw now, as never before I
had seen so plainly, that each as he walked
constantly turned to catch the whispers of a
spectre at his ear, the spectre of Uncertainty.
'Do your work ever so well,' the spectre was
whispering — 'rise early and toil till late, rob
cunningly or serve faithfully, you shall never
know security. Rich you may be and still came to
poverty at last. Leave ever so much wealth to your
children, you cannot buy the assurance that your
son may not be the servant of your servant, or
that your daughter will not have to sell herself
for bread.'"

And what about the Poor? And what about Charity?
Both would disappear as even the very poor of all
the Earth would be raised up to the high living
standard that technology could provide. The old
and the invalid would be taken care of and,
because they do not fear for their future, would
be able to continue, or in some cases, begin, to
play a useful role in our Society.

Some people advocate taking away from the rich and
sharing with the poor. But that would not do very
much to end the world's poverty. We must instead
create new wealth. This we can do through the
means already described: Technology, peace, and
the sane use of the Earth's resources. Again, as
Edward Bellamy wrote in his novel 'Looking
Backward':

"I told them that I had not meant to accuse them, as if they, or the rich in general, were responsible for the misery of the world. True indeed it was, that the superfluity which they wasted would, otherwise bestowed, relieve much bitter suffering. These costly viands, these rich wines, these gorgeous fabrics and glistening jewels represented the ransom of many lives. They were verily not without the guiltiness of those who waste in a land stricken with famine. Nevertheless, all the waste of all the rich, were it saved, would go but a little way to cure the poverty of the world. There was so little to divide that even if the rich went to share with the poor, there would be but a common fare of crusts, albeit made very sweet then by brotherly love."

THE ROLE OF ADVERTISING

Advertising is very important in today's society because of our competitive economy. But advertising is not necessarily good. Each day, according to Vance Packard in his book 'The Waste Makers', each American is subject to over 1100 advertisements. They are everywhere: on television, on the radio, billboards, buses, taxis, in neon lights on the front of stores, even on litter baskets and in newspapers.

Trees are made into newspapers. Living trees are made into newspapers. The average newspaper is over 2/3 advertisements. And most of the news isn't very good anyway.

Advertising, by its own admission, produces 'discontent'. Advertisers have, in fact, discovered that audiences are more apt to buy their product if the TV shows they sponsor have violence and chaos in them, than if the shows have no violence and portray positive human values. The more discontent – the greater sales of products.

Advertisers will often tell you that their latest product will make you happy or successful or well loved. If you happen to be poor or think that you are, you still want to be happy. And if this product promises you happiness and you don't have the money to buy it – perhaps you might be willing to steal the product or steal the money to buy it. And 'rich' people steal as much as do the 'poor' – even though the nature of their thievery may be more complex and less obvious.

It is becoming increasingly apparent to many that happiness cannot reasonably be found in things exterior to ourselves. Happiness comes from within. Happiness could develop easily in a society which promotes positive human values.

Happiness could develop easily in a society which promotes positive human values. Happiness is more difficult to develop in a society which reminds you how unhappy you are without this or that latest product.

In our Utopia, people would soon see the 'blind alley' of owning things. Possession would be seen to be burdensome. People, freed from insecurity and from having to worry about "how to earn a living" would be happier with less material things. The less we own, the greater our freedom. William James once wrote that "lives based on having are less free than lives based on doing or being."

In conclusion, let us say that advertising could be used to humankind's advantage. People involved in advertising are some of the most creative on the planet. Their insights into human behavior can be of great assistance in teaching people new values and inspiring people to new achievements. Such could be the way they could contribute to our Utopia.

POPULATION

Population is a major problem in our world today and so is the continued ecological destruction of our Earth environment and the inequitable distribution of our Earth resources by the wealthy nations and peoples of the world at the expense of the poor nations and peoples. The fear of overpopulation should not be allowed to stop the development of courageous, creative, and innovative policies indispensable to overcoming the challenges of world poverty and the mal-distribution of the world's wealth.

When any society moves toward high education standards and high standard of living, the people in that society tend to have fewer children. This has been true of the United States, Canada, Western Europe, Australia, and Japan. As the rest of the world's living standard is raised, their birth rates will more than likely drop also.

Buckminster Fuller does not feel that there is a population problem. He says the whole of present humanity can presently stand in the room that makes up greater New York City. He says that there is "more than enough to go around" for everyone once we have utilized technology and ended war.

He says that it is our mission to populate the Universe.

In our Utopia, the major emphasis would be upon the practice of voluntary birth control. Abortions would be available but would be discouraged in favor of birth control, loving communities, and liberal adoption policies.

It is expected that most people would almost automatically favor smaller families and the increased freedom for parents that smaller families allow.

FOOD AND AGRICULTURE

In our Utopia, we will grow our food as naturally as possible. Where possible we will eliminate pesticide and insecticide sprays and grow our foods in accordance with Nature.

One major problem with spraying is that insects and rodents considered harmful are rapidly becoming immune to the sprays; thus dosages must continually be increased and new poisons invented. The spraying of these poisons is ruining the food-growing potential of the land, polluting the ground waters, killing birds, killing helpful insects, and may even be having long-term genetic effects on human beings.

Chemical fertilizers also cause problems. They kill earthworms. Earthworms are extremely important: They bore through the soil, thereby impregnating it with air and permitting water to penetrate the earth and not runoff. This prevents soil erosion. Though chemical fertilizers speed up plant growth, they reduce the humus fertility in the soil until the land actually dies.

It makes more sense to grow organically without the use of chemicals and in accordance with the biological laws found in the Balance of Nature. This is the way food will be produced in our Utopia.

Strong plants, well fertilized with natural fertilizers, will repel bugs. In fact, bugs usually only attack the weaker pants anyway. There are more insects in the world than there are people. So we had better learn to coexist with them.

If we find we must control a species of insect, then instead of chemicals we will continue to move to 'biological control'. Entomologists, those scientists who specialize in insect behavior, have bred male insects of various species who are sterile but yet sexually aggressive. These male insects will seek out females of their species and breed with them. The female will have a 'false pregnancy' and will avoid other potent males of the species, but she will bear no offspring. This is quite an imaginative way to remove troublesome insect problems.

Food production would still be mechanized in our Utopia. Our technology will not neglect agriculture. But this mechanization would be in accordance with the ecology of each region and the ecology of each crop and not just for increased profits.

Farms will have a variety of plant life, both as a means of controlling pests and the spread of infectious plant diseases, as well as to enhance scenic beauty.

Produce will be rushed from the farms to all food centers while it is fresh and wholesome. Limited additives and limited preservatives will be used. There will be no deceptive advertising of foods.

Food distribution will be guided by computers and food distribution will be Earthwide. The computers will indicate where there are needs for food and also where this food is available. No longer will artificial boundaries serve to restrict trade. And no longer will food rot because there are only limited transportation methods to move food where it is needed and belongs.

In addition to the farms, all Earth People would be encouraged to set up small family and larger community gardens. Gardening experts would be readily available to help people in their garden projects. People would be readily available to help others in their garden projects. People would also be encouraged to plant fruit and nut trees in their backyards and to plant the front of their homes in gardens as well as grass. These home gardens will probably have the highest productive yield per acre of all agricultural land due to the personal involvement of the growers.

Green Spaces would be reserved in the cities for food production and even for woods and forests. Farming would move back into the city and every person would experience a link with the soil and the world of nature. Cities would be literally turned into gardens. Cities will become more humane. They may become smaller in size and people will enjoy the friendliness and trust still found today in small town life.

Geomancy, the scientific and artful expression of fundamental geophysical and biophysical laws on the Earth, would come into its own. Geomancers, using intuitive intelligence, attempt to divine the hidden meaning and relate the key points of mutual harmony in the land, together with the influences that different areas have on plants, animals, and mankind. No longer would housing and 'development' projects destroy our best food growing lands or destroy the last mating areas of an endangered bird species.

Irrigation projects of a major scale will reclaim the Earth's deserts and barren places. Infertile lands will be brought back to fertility through extensive composting and the use of natural fertilizers. Forests will be replanted all over the Earth and sanctuaries for animals will be made secure.

HYDROPONICS

We will turn increasingly to Hydroponics, which refers to water, sand, or gravel culture, tank farming, and chemi-culture. Basically, hydroponics involves growing plants without using soil. Instead, another medium – water, gravel, sand, and the like – is used in which plants grow, being 'fed' by a nutrient solution which contains all the elements the plants need for development.

Hydroponics frees plants from soil, thus lessening the problems of insects and weed control. It also liberates plants from the energy drain involved in pushing roots through the soil.

Moreover, the plant doesn't need to grow as elaborate a root system because the roots have easy access to what they need – water and nutrients – through the solution in which they are suspended.

MEAT EATING

I am not a vegetarian but I am told that meat eating is ecologically unsound. A cow must be fed twenty-one pounds of non-meat foods in order to produce just one pound of meat protein for human consumption. This is a tremendous waste of corn, wheat, oats, barley, soybeans, and land area just to produce beef.

According to the Dean of Agriculture of Ohio State University, 35 percent more food would be available for human consumption if food were available directly to humans rather than fed through animals as a "middle producer." Indeed, one half of the harvested agricultural land in the United States is devoted to feed crops for animals. Between one-third and one-half of the North American continental land surface is used for animal grazing.

Fish are also used as animal feed. According to an official in the Food and Agricultural Organization of the United Nations, half of the world fish catch was being turned into meal for pigs and chickens. Less than 15 percent, at best, of this input reappears as meat that is available for human consumption. Most of this fish product is being shipped to North America and Western Europe from the underdeveloped, protein-poor nations, particularly in Latin America. That means that the poorer nations are supporting the extravagant food habits of the rich nations - and going hungry themselves.

Animals are mistreated in the process of breeding them for market. They are force-fed, pumped with antibiotics and growth hormones, and kept in overcrowded housing conditions. Animals are looked upon, not as entities unto themselves, but as so much merchandise. Each year in the U.S. alone, it is estimated that one billion animals, including fish, are slaughtered for our dining tables.

In our Utopia, people could eat meat if they wished, but would be encouraged to move toward non-meat meals as much as possible. After all, the practice of vegetarianism seems more in keeping with the humaneness which our Utopia seeks to develop.

Moreover, we find that non-meat food sources, when combined, can easily and economically satisfy our need for complete proteins. For example, beans and rice, make a good protein complement; as do seeds and milk. A really excellent book describing combinations of non-meat proteins to produce complete protein value is 'Diet for a Small Planet' by Francis Moore Lappe, published by Friends of the Earth and Ballantine Books. This book also goes into detail about the non-ecological aspects of meat eating.

In our Utopia all animals, including feed animals, would be treated with respect even until the moment they die. There will be no more overcrowded cattle feed lots of forced feeding of geese to make their livers bigger.

NEW SOURCES OF PROTEIN
FOR HUMAN CONSUMPTION

Buckminster Fuller calls attention to new protein
discoveries in '*I Seem to be A Verb*':

"Two prodigious, making-the-world-work
breakthroughs in late 1969. Weeds and leaves can
now be converted into a protein food that has the
same consistency as cheese. Animal blood can now
be converted into a substance that tastes a
little like powdered milk and is 50 percent
protein. (More than 2,000,000,000 pounds of
animal bloow are thrown away every year in the
United States alone)."

ALTERNATIVE FEEDS FOR ANIMALS

Future estimates are that there will be meat around
for those who want it, thanks to Alternative Feeds.
Raw sewage, when treated by certain
micro-organisms, can be converted into a rich
protein feed. Agricultural experts have even
devised ways to feed animals through processing
urea and cow manure into animal feed products.
Reports are that animals react favorably to such
feed.

The reason that manure can be re-used is that
despite its four stomachs, a cow's digestive
system is rather inefficient. The semisolid wastes
and other cellulose materials in manure contain
nutrients to make this process worthwhile. The
result is a feed that is comparable to high grade
alfalfa.

In the United States there are about 1.7 billion

tons of animal waste produced each year, and three-quarters of that is cow manure. Conversion of this waste would provide a cheap animal feed and would eliminate an acute problem of animal feed lot pollution caused by so much waste concentrated in one place, thus contaminating land and water.

Researchers with the U.S. Department of Agriculture estimate that the recovery for feed on only one-third of the U.S. animal waste would produce as much protein as is contained in the country's annual soybean crop.

IN CONSIDERATION OF ANIMALS

In our Utopia, many parts of zoos would close down as would menageries and circuses, as animals are resettled in their natural habitats and in well protected and maintained animal reserves. Is it really necessary to train bears and elephants to walk on their back legs and twirl balls – just to satisfy peoples' need for amusement.

If, for example, people wished to see real penguins, they could go to the South Pole and visit with them in a surrounding where the penguins were living naturally rather than in trained 'performance', Perhaps the penguins would welcome them and put them up in their homes and hearts and treat them as their brothers and sisters!

Every animal would maintain its own integrity of life. We would find there is more than enough space to go around for both people and numerous varieties of animal, bird, fish, and plant life. A natural balance in nature would be restored.

Instead of today's zoos, where real animals are held captive and displayed, holographic effects would be developed which would present large visual and 3-D effects of animals as they appear in their native habitats. Holography is art / technology which records, stores, and replays a visual scene by high resolution photography of laser beam interference pattern causes the original photographed object to become visible in three dimensions.

HUNTING

Hunters generally have a special relationship to, a special love of Nature that many of us have not acquired. They are involved in Nature. Hunting, therefore, of non-endangered animal species, under specific regulations, would be permitted. Perhaps people in our Utopia would evolve away from hunting as time goes on.

THE WEARING OF ANIMAL FURS

The wearing of furs, produced from fur-bearing animals, would be discouraged 'Fake' or synthetic furs can be just as fashionable and much more practical. The slaughter of baby seals for their skins would certainly stop.

FORESTS, LUMBER, AND PAPER PRODUCTS

It has become obvious to many people that tree

paper and the raw timber it is derived from are coming into short supply.

In our Utopia, we would conserve and recycle paper. Currently only 20% of newsprint is recycled. In our Society, we would aim to recycle all paper. Newspapers, per se, would probably come close to disappearing as there would be so little 'bad news' to report, and advertising as we know it would become a thing of the past. Most of our present day paperwork would be stored in computers and would be available by computer. Books would be microfilmed: to read a 'book' you'll choose the appropriate CD which you would then insert into a slot in a computer screen terminal, and it would flash on your screen. To turn the 'page' you merely touch a button. The need for paper would be replaced largely by CD's.

Packaging which is now down in paper bags would be replaced by sturdy, reusable cloth bags. Cardboard box packaging would be replaced by sturdy reusable lightweight plastic boxes.

In the event there is a limited need for paper products, small 'timber farms' would be established, based on the 30 year cutting and reforestation cycle of timberland. But, in reality, the need for paper and paper products would diminish considerably.

Our world forests would be preserved for human visitation, animal habitation and for the important job they do in soil conservation.

We could also move towards hemp as a paper source. Hemp paper is sturdier, more longlasting than tree paper and 4 times as many paper products can be produced from an acre fof hemp than an acre of tree paper. And it is much more ecologically sound.

STAYING HEALTHY

Over the last 100 years, life expectancy has been
increasing dramatically. Reasons for our increased
longevity have been society's improvements in
hygiene: garbage collections, sewage disposals,
pumped-in-water, inoculations, improved and
increasingly widespread personal cleansing habits,
improved medical procedures, and alternative
healthcare.

Interestingly enough, future declines in longevity
may happen due to society's inability or refusal
to maintain the improved hygienic standards:
increasingly polluted waters, the question of waste
and sewage disposals, dirty air. This was clearly
visible in the cholera epidemic of Southern Italy
during the middle part of 1973, caused by the
eating of contaminated shellfish from the polluted
coastal waters off the Italian coastline. Perhaps
this is yet another forecast of things to come if
we do not work to clean up our environment.

Today we find that degenerative diseases are
beginning to take their toll of persons at
younger and younger ages. Stress, pollution,
smoking habits, and diet are the main causes for
this decline. In addition, the human body is
having to cope with an increasing range of drugs
and food additives, many of which are adequately
tested before being marketed.

How would our Utopia change things so that we
would lead longer, healthier lives?

First, we would REDUCE, by all means thus far
discussed in this book, most, if not all, for the
stressful conditions in life.

Second, POLLUTION; with its harmful effects, would be eliminated.

Third, DIET REFORM.

Diet reform would play a large part in our Utopia, even as it is today, among increasing numbers of enlightened and concerned people. People would be encouraged to move away from processed foods loaded with preservatives, stabilizers, emulsifiers, etc. They would return to natural foods. As we return to natural foods, disease rates would go down, and we would live longer, healthier lives. Education and application of sound nutritional habits would be encouraged.

Fourth, HEALING ARTS.

Preventative medicine, 'keeping people well', would be encouraged through the use of scientific nutrition, natural hygiene, sound exercise programs, and positive mind and thought control.

If a person did become ill, he or she would be entitled to the best medical and healing arts available. These services would be provided for free, as would hospital and recuperative care. No longer would any person be denied the best healthcare because of a lack of income. A major emphasis in our Utopia would be in keeping people well.

We would return to the herbal remedies of our fore-parents. We would encourage the study and application of various forms of massage therapy and acupuncture. Chiropractic and naturopathic care would come into their own.

Reaching the age of 120, or even higher, would be a 'natural occurrence' in our Utopia.

HEALING CENTERS

Society today is filled with fear and anger. Too many people feel that it is natural to explode in angry blows and words with one another. They react this way because of their previous environmental conditioning. But we are moving into a new Society where feelings of fear, anger, and jealousy should no longer exist.

And as we move towards our new society, we should set up Centers, where people can come for Dealing. We try not to be angry with the polluter of today nor the war patriot. They are misguided. They have not opened their consciousness to become aware that this is really a beautiful world. These people are still Earth People, as are you and I. We must help them by being ready to receive them with open and comforting arms when they realize the futility of their past ways and seek cleansing for their past actions. We must encourage them and love them. And we must also set up centers for our own continued evolution and creativity.

These Centers would also be Centers for Creativity and Growth, for Human Dynamics and Human Potential. Perhaps it will be through group sensitivity, massage, or the human touch; yoga or zen; through bio-feedback machines, or Reichian therapy; positive thinking and programming; meditating; or through a re-education in moral and religious thinking, allowing each person to see the Christ-Buddha perfection within themselves.

Eventually, the need for these Centers will disappear, as the entire Society becomes open, trusting, and loving. Expressions of Self would be a part of everyday life.

NUTRITION

Our Utopian Society would encourage and promote sound nutritional values. Its incredible to think how many people are being deliberately malnourished in America today thanks to the confused efforts of the food industry. This industry seems to be only interested in profits. They are attempting to consolidate their market and remove all natural foods from our plates and replace them with processed ones.

The processed foods, those which are rich in refined and modified carbohydrates like white flour, are probably major causes of diabetes, heart and arterial disease, and intestinal cancer, among other ailments. Our Utopian Society cannot afford the illness and early death of so many of its members thanks to bad nutrition.

Rather than banning these foods – a sound nutritional system would soon bring demand for these foods to a minimum. All foods would be rated according to their nutritional value on a plus -minus scale. Dr. Michael Jacobson has written a book detailing this scheme. In his 'Nutritional Scoreboards: Your Guide to Better Eating', published by the Center for Science in the Public Interest.

Dr. Jacobson writes:

"People have to learn they get things other than just enjoyment from food. They need continuous education and complete information to make wise buying decisions, then if they still select a poor diet, it's their own problem."

As long as today's society continues to throw away the best parts of its wheat, rice, potatoes, and continues to devote millions of acres to the growing of non-foods such as sugar, instead of food for peoples' bellies – so will the Earth have starving people.

SNOWMOBILING AND MULTI-TERRAIN VEHICLES

Two forms of recreation must come to an end if our environment is going to survive: the first is motor boating using the internal combustion engine, and the second is multi-terrain vehicles.

Motor boating, in fact, all boats ships, barges, and tugs, which use the internal combustion engine, add too much fuel exhaust and too much spilled gas and oil to waterways. The fish cannot breathe. The water is becoming unfit for people to swim in and to drink from. Remember what we learned earlier about our fragile continental shelves.

Sail boating or motor boating which use alternative, non-polluting energy sources seem perfectly okay.

Snowmobiling destroys the sanctity of our forests and other natural areas. It uproots small trees and vegetation, making it difficult for deer and

other animals to feed during the winter months.
Snowmobiling, with its internal combustion engine,
also brings pollution to the woodlands. Sometimes
snowmobilers use their machines to 'run' animals
into exhaustion and death.

Snowmobiling and all such multi-terrain vehicles
must be restrained as recreation and used only
where they are needed as the major form of people
transportation such as in Northern Canada.
Perhaps, when these vehicles use alternative,
non-polluting energy sources, special runs could
be developed for their use. Maybe we could
simply revitalize the good old fashioned horse and
sleigh.

AMUSEMENTS

Violence in movies and on television would
disappear as the market for such diversion fades
out. Violence in media encourages some people in
society to be violent also. Much of this violence
is geared by media to sell products. Violence for
commercial purposes would disappear in our
Utopia.

Finally, we would say that a large aspect of our
educational system would be to educate people into
how to utilize their increasing amounts of leisure
time.

Buckminster Fuller talks about the "win win" game,
where everybody wins. This is the way our future
Society would be set up and this would be the game
we would all be playing in our Utopia.

A PRIMITIVE RESPECT FOR NATURE

Some people hold the Biblical injunction found in Genesis 1:28, and its misapplication by so many Christians as the basis of much of Western man's ecological problems: "And God blessed them, and God said unto them, be fruitful and multiply, and replenish the earth, and subdue it: and have dominion over the fish of the sea, and over the fowl of the air, and over every living thing that moveth upon the earth."

Many believed that this injunction allowed man to do whatever he wished with this world. Unfortunately, many still believe this today.

This viewpoint is far removed from the primitive and the animistic religious view of man which sees man as a part, but not particularly the primary dominating life force, of Nature.

Many of the 'primitive' peoples of both yesterday and today seem to have a greater respect for and a working relationship with Nature. They believe that a spirit inhabits all life forms, including trees and grasses, and bodies of water. This system of belief is called 'animism'. According to this belief, it is wrong to do harm to living entities. If, for example, 'primitive' persons cut down a tree for its wood, they will first 'ask' (pray to) the tree for forgiveness.

The early Greeks accepted 'pantheism', or the belief that God is always present in every phenomenon.

A view similar to this is expressed in Carlos Castenada's book, 'Journey to Ixtlan,' If you wished to eat a plant, you first speak to the plant and explain to it that you yourself expect to be surrendered up to a Higher Power, at some later time, just as you expect the plant to surrender itself for your survival now.

While such 'primitive' views could be perhaps seen as delaying 'progress' and man's ability to affect Nature, perhaps modern man has moved too heavily in the opposite direction – toward the destruction of Nature, rather than living in harmony with it.

LANGUAGE

In our One Earth Utopia, each ethnic group could continue to speak their own language as they wished. Additionally, we would encourage the use of a universal Earth language.

In 1887, a Polish language professor, Dr. Zamenhof, developed such a language. He wrote under the name of Dr. Esperanto, "one who hopes?" Groups of people all over the Earth already speak Esperanto.

Perhaps in our Utopia we would use Esperanto, or we could develop an even better Earth language. Buckminster Fuller has suggested that we place all Earth languages and dialects in a computer and then let the computer compute the language which would be most familiar to Earth people.

INTENTIONAL COMMUNITIES

Just as tribal and native peoples would be

encouraged and allowed to maintain their tribal life, other groups of people would be allowed to set up their own ecological or 'intentional communities'. These communities could choose their own lifestyles, educational systems, work and economic systems, as they wished.

Such a community would be established after careful study has been made of a land area's natural ecology: water and air resources, climate, geological formations, raw materials, solid, and natural flora and fauna. The population of the community would be limited by conscious design to the ecological capacity of the region. Land management would be guided by ecological principles so that and equilibrium is maintained between the human inhabitants and these natural factors.

These communities would also be able to tune in to the Earthwide community for energy sources or trade of whatever they wished to the extent that they wished. Or else they could be entirely on their own, living off the land.

Murray Bookchin, an anarchist ecologist, suggests that technology could be scaled to community levels and that factories could be easily and continually converted to produce the changing material goods needed by a small community of people as the need for each product arises. Each community would be able to gather its own energy through solar energy or similar alternative energy sources scaled to receive just enough energy to keep the community self-sufficient and independent of outside sources.

The intentional communities must make assurances

that they will live peacefully and harmoniously with everyone else and will not propagate ideas of ethnocentrism, suggesting that their particular group is better than others. They would be free to do their 'thing' and must let other groups not similarly inclined to 'do their own thing' also.

Having many of these intentional communities would permit experimentation and introduction of new ideas which, if they work on a small community basis, could be adopted by the society as a whole.

Presently communal living arrangements are seemingly discouraged by our political and economic leaders. They would like us to keep our defined family units, the 'nuclear' family rather than an 'extended' one. In this way, more individual houses, televisions, washing machines, etc., are sold. When a group of people live together this cuts down on their consumption of so many materials.

A second beneficial aspect of people living together, means, that they have many opportunities to learn to adjust to one another. There is little room for grouches in a communal setting. As people adjust to many different personalities within the home commune, then their ability to adjust to different personalities outside the home also increases.

We live in a world of people. Within the communal setting, interaction takes place in a friendly manner. If one commune member has a problem adjusting, the group can work it out with him or her. The individual is then more prepared to enter the outside world.

For grouches to just grouch by themselves separated in their own little 'castle', brooding with their neuroses means that they may carry their neuroses with them when they step out their front door and then all society will suffer. In a communal setting people learn to interact with one another, share with one another, and break down barriers. Successful communal living is a successful life learning process.

In urban areas as well as rural ones, communes could be large structures having many shared space areas: TV rooms, kitchen facilities, laundry facilities, and workshops. Within the commune, each person could have their own rooms also. The communes could be supported by small factories, or craft work, farming, or by people having jobs in the outside community.

It is important to note: communal living is an option, most people will continue to live as they always have, in their own homes and with their own families, and that would be 100% OK!

ALTERNATIVE LIFESTYLES

In our Utopia we continue to move to establish new lifestyles just as so many people of all ages are already doing today. Indeed, it is because of the changing lifestyles and developing new consciousness that we can even suggest that our Utopia would come about.

Our Utopian lifestyles would allow for personal freedom, personal development, personal fulfillment. We cannot own people nor can we stop change. We cannot control the lives of our

children, our wives, our husbands, or our
neighbors.

In our future society, individuals would be
encouraged to examine alternative lifestyles to
check out their respective merits. Our advancing
technology and leisure time will allow for more
diversity in lifestyle not for more conformity.

In an earlier society, everyone had to struggle
just to stay alive. There was no room for anyone
who would not stay within the small groups limited
norms. In our future society and today, there is
so much more room and freedom to choose one's path
for one's self. The society of the Scandinavian
countries allows full freedom for alternative
living styles for those who want them. Perhaps
more research should be available about the
success or struggles of these ventures.

CHILDREN IN OUR FUTURE SOCIETY

A significant characteristic of our Utopia is that
children would not be taught - nor would they have
examples to observe the social myths and
prejudices that most adults have grown up with and
have had to struggle to overcome. Children would
be raised in an era free from hate, war and greed.
They would not have to contend for supremacy in
the marketplace or survival on the battlefield.

Just as adults can set up their own intentional
communities, communes and such, children would
perhaps be able to set up their own children's
houses. Their houses would contain real
furniture scaled to size for the children. Foods
such as breads, cereals, nourishing liquids,

fruits, seeds, nuts, and other foods easily eaten without hot preparation could be available for children wishing to eat on their own.

Having children's houses would permit children to choose to be by themselves, and also allow them to interact in the grown-up community when they wished to do so.

As socialization in the community would encourage and reflect positive relationships among people, bullying and other forms of anti-social behavior would have little reinforcement and would thus be less unlikely to develop among children.

Schooling would be free-flowing and experimental. Every effort would be made to encourage rather than stifle it.

Many 'Earthparents' would share the nurturing of their 'Earthchildren' ...Perhaps all Earthchildren would consider all Earthmen and Earthwomen as their 'parents', and all Earthparents would feel love and caring and responsibility for all Earthchildren.

Aldous Huxley, in his book 'Island', suggests that children should be provided with many sets of parents, to whose homes they could visit and stay for any length of time. In this way they would be exposed to many new environments and lifestyles and also have a place to go to "cool it" from their biological parents, if things got too rough on the home scene, for either the parents or the children.

The "facts of life" should not be concealed from, nor misrepresented to children. They would receive clear and honest information about anatomy and sex when they request it. Children growing up in this environment would be free from sexual guild and hang-ups, and should enter into personal sexual relationships more knowingly and confidently.

Affection and love would be generously bestowed on Earthchildren. As these children grow up, they would continue to see our society burgeoning out and becoming ever more loving, responsive and perfect as yet more and more children grow up unhampered by the chaos of yesterday and begin to structure their lives in increasingly free-flowing, loving and creative ways.

As Buckminster Fuller writes:

"Our children and their children are our future days. If we do not comprehend and realize our potential ability to support all life forever we are cosmically bankrupt."

EDUCATION

The word 'education', comes from the Latin root 'educare', which means to "bring forth". 'Education' means the "bringing forth" of that which is already within a person.

Buckminster Fuller says that all children are born geniuses: All children have the "genius capacity." But in the case of 99 of our 100, this genius capacity is programmed out of them before they reach the age of six. This is generally because they are 'shut up', their questions ignored, or their imagination stifled.

Let us examine how this might happen:

Sally (age 4) asks her father: "Daddy, where did I come from?" Father, embarrassed, replies; "Go ask your mother."

Johnny (age 6) is sitting in school at a desk for six long hours daily. The teachers is running on about arithmetic or patriotism or something. But Johnny's attention is really outside the classroom. In his mind, he is playing ball or imagining a sand castle. The teacher observes Johnny and says sharply, "Johnny, stop daydreaming. Come back to reality."

No, education in our Utopia must be different. Education would seek to add to the genius capacity of children rather than take it away.

I do not assume to have all the answers. I have been an educator for almost 50 years. Here are only a few of my ideas as they apply to a formal education system:

Education would be a joyous affair. Classes would be small. Teachers would be employed for their creative ability. Students would not be compelled to attend school, but would do so because they felt it to be a valuable experience. Grading and testing, which often encourage cut throat competition, cheating, and neurosis, and is aimed at preparing students for the present 'there is not enough to go around' society, would be eliminated. Students would study and learn because they wanted to, not because they had to. Summerhill, an experimental school established by A.S. Neill, is a great example.

Students would take classes in art, creative dance, and in many forms of artistic expression. Classes in philosophy would be available as well as discussion classes in values. Students would learn about the great teachers of our Earth Heritage.

In order to implement the overall Utopian design of our society, a moral code would be developed based upon the moral principles we would like to see built up in our Utopia. I consider these principles to be Love, Truth, Sharing, and Compassion.

There would be emphasis on classes in hygiene, nutrition, and physical culture – gymnastics and yoga, as well as, art, music, and technology. There would be courses in how to get along with other people, self-expression, and self-fulfillment.

Technology and science instruction would not be neglected. Students would learn the underlying principles operating in our Universe.

Specialization would initially be discouraged in order to allow students the ability to look at the Earth as a whole eco-system. A working middle-ground would be set up between a general overview on the one hand and the specialization society needs for it to function at an optimum in a technological era on the other.

The educational system would be set up so as to provide students with the opportunity to travel all over the Earth, either by themselves or in organized groups. They would visit various cultures, 'native peoples,' and time zones. They would view museums and archeological ruins and restorations. They would also visit factories, textile mills, power plants, shipbuilding docks, farms, ranches, computer centers, and so forth. In this way every student would have a broad working knowledge of our Earth home and its broad heritage as well as a first hand understanding of many of the various occupations of our Earth economy.

Education would be a life long process. Schools would offer a variety of classes for all age groups. All education would be free of charge. And education would not only prepare people for jobs and vocational skills, but would also prepare them with ideas for creative uses of their increasingly large amount of leisure time.

Education would not be limited to schools alone. Lecture halls, perhaps called Earth Centers, where issues could be examined and debated would emerge all across the Earth. Community Centers where people could join together in shared projects, such as singing, dance, art, sports, would also be encouraged. We would also see the emergence of Healing Centers, of Centers of Living and Interacting, which would provide numerous avenues for people to solve personal and interpersonal problems as well as full self-development and awareness.

Our Educational System would be fluid and innovative. It would reduce as much as possible any distinctions and distances between student and teacher. We would all be 'Students of Life'. Buckminster Fuller suggests that we all be given full time "Fellowships to Think". He suggests that the ideas and breakthroughs of just one person out of 100,000 would more than likely pay for the Fellowships of the other 99,999.

And so geniuses we are born, and, thanks to our Utopian education system, geniuses we remain.

RELIGION AND RELIGIOUS FREEDOM

THE EARTH CHURCH

There is a great spiritual awakening on the part of many people today. This is manifested by interest in many areas of Eastern Though and its Western Application: Vendata of India; Taoism; Buddhism; Zen; Yoga in all its forms; Meditation; Silva Mind Control; Living the life and works of Jesus Christ; Living the communal, agrarian life; Urban Communes; and living the life of the American Indian (the 'native peoples'). Through Tai Chi, Sufi dancing, and Rudolf Steiner's eurhythmy, people are learning to meditate with their whole bodies.

Youth are giving up their pursuit of material things and are searching for and finding meaning and happiness within themselves. Men and women are studying their role in the Universe and finding that we are all of the same spirit. Materialism is giving way to metaphysics and personal fulfillments.

Maybe it's in the stars. After all, "This is the dawning of the age of Aquarius". Maybe we ARE supposed to save ourselves. Certainly our species is in an evolutionary process. Utopia is our right and our heritage. The Bible reads: "Come, beloved of my right hand, and receive the inheritance I have prepared for you since the foundation of the world."

Too often in the past religious systems, while starting out with positive promises, have fallen from their high ideals and teachings into set patterns of dogma, ritual, superstition, material gain, and the idea that their religion is the 'only way' to 'Salvation', i.e., 'Enlightenment'. Perhaps this is changing today. In our Utopia all of the world's religious systems would be encouraged to continue the move toward Ecumenism and common Brother and Sisterhood. Hopefully, just as individuals are moving toward Godhead, the world's religions would move in these directions too.

In our Utopia, freedom of religion as well as the freedom to not believe in any organized faith or in any faith at all would coexist. Many people would continue, however, to go beyond all of the different dogmas and rituals of the varying religions in order to get to the underlying core of all.

In our Utopia, we would come to understand our universe and would know ourselves as one with it. We would substitute Mind for Ritual. Indeed, it would be through the power of Mind that the best aspects of our Utopia will come forth. We will be able to program and project for our future. We will continually design a better world through the imagination and intuitive powers of our minds.

And as we establish the perfect society our Godlike qualities would come forth. Fuller writes, "So I find that everybody is getting to be an Einstein or a Christ, finding principles and understanding."

Perhaps a new Earthwide religion will emerge that

will unite all Earth people together, a religion which will not have one Prophet, but six billion, a religion of mind, rationality, science, technology, faith, sharing, and love. A religion which does not claim holy cities or shrines, but sees, in face, the whole Earth and the whole Universe and everything in it as suitable to be called Holy and therefore respected and loved.

Such would be the Earth Church and we would all be its priests, mullahs, and prophets.

CITIES

TEAR UP THE CONCRETE AND LET THE EARTH BREATHE

Can the cities be made livable or are cities inherently unlivable? The answer, of course, is that cities within our Utopia could be made livable if significant alterations are made in their present structures.

Presently most cities are too spread out, too impersonal, too congested, and too choked by pollution. Urban sprawl threatens to destroy much of our farmland. Many areas of cities are unsafe to walk either by day or night and residents live in fear of each other. There are inadequate parks and green spaces for city residents to be able to feel any relationship with Nature and the natural environment. The bright lights of the city by night block out the ease of seeing the glitter of the stars in the Heavens.

As people are freed from the necessity of 'earning a living', and machines do more and more of our work, then people would be freed from having to live in the cities in order to be close to their work. As people leave the cities to resettle in the countryside and in small towns and villages – many houses, apartments, and office buildings could be torn down and greenery established in their place.

But yet not all older homes and other buildings must be torn down. We would make a conscious effort to save and preserve the most notable pieces of architecture of each architectural period of each geographical region which are still in existence.

If it is considered necessary to build new housing units then we would utilize 'organic' architecture. Housing units would be built in a natural setting nestled among the trees and vegetation, merged into the greenery. They could be carved out of rock or dug into the earth.

Paolo Soleri, a visionary thinker and architect, proposes "arcology". By his definition, architecture and ecology are two parts of the same thing. This, he calls, "arcology".

Soleri proposes the centralization of society far beyond conventional urban planners' concepts of density. By his plan, hundreds of thousands of people would live in intense and orderly concentration within a few square miles. This would leave the surrounding land basically unoccupied and available to all.

Arcosanti is the name of the new town which Soleri and his students and friends are currently developing on a mesa in north central Arizona. Compact multi-layered, three dimensional, it will be the first environment designed according to the principles of arcology.

Anyone interested in roughing it at the site, and not adverse to hard work, can apply to join a six-week workshop.

Write:

Paolo Soleri, Cosanti Foundation, 6433 Doubletree Road, Scottsdale, AZ 85253.

Soleri's image is the exact opposite of Greek planner Doxiadis's "ecumenopolis", the oozing urbanism relentlessly covering whole continents. This terrible destruction of the land should not be in our future. We would build high and down under rather than spread outward. We would try to keep as much open land available as possible. Apartments are very much utilized in Europe today. Many people live in sturdy, well kept, and spacious apartment houses rather than in individual homes on private lots as in the United States.

Buckminster Fuller proposes both Domed Cities and Geodeisic Domes for homes and buildings as ways to make the cities more livable and to preserve energy and material resources. Geodeisic domes are igloo shaped. According to Fuller, they are the most economical housing units and provide the greatest area of living space using the least amount of materials. They are easily movable and readily adapt to solar heating power. They are also resistant to extreme weather conditions, such as, hurricanes and tornados.

Buckminster Fuller has also proposed that major cities be domed over. He says that the cost of these domes would be paid for in just ten years with the amount we would save from just not having to pay for snow removal from city streets.

The domes would be high and their structural members so delicate that they would appear to be invisible. They would keep out rain, snow, storms, and industrial fumes. They would collect rain water as it drains from the sides and convey this relatively clean water to large storage reservoirs to be used by the city as needed. According to

Fuller, the domes would reduce energy losses in winter heating and summer cooling to one eighty-fifth of the present cost. The domes would operate as a controlled cloud, bringing shadow when shadow is desirable, allowing sun when sun is desired.

The domed city would not only be practical, but aesthetically pleasing. Covered streets could have outdoor restaurants year round. Windows could be open. Gardens would bloom all year long. People could live in gardens, or upon garden terraced skyscrapers, needing only local screening for privacy.

Domes could also be used for occupations of deserts, the inhabitation of the Arctic and the Antarctic, and to cover archaeological sites, especially those which should be preserved as historical monuments.

Within our Utopia, some cities would be small enough so that the residents would sense the friendliness and trust that still exists in many small towns even today. Crime and violence would disappear as each person's economic needs were met and the harsh conditions in the cities were transformed into beauty and space.

Cities would become centers of aesthetic beauty as mass transit replaced autos. The streets could be replaced as walkways, gardens, and park benches took their place. The expressways and freeways could be flooded and fish and bird life moved in. Canoes, rafts, and slow moving barges would move people and material goods at a leisurely pace throughout the metropolitan areas.

Art forms would not only be displayed in museums but would be all over the cities and countryside. Each block could have its own sculptures. Works of art would decorate outsides and insides of most buildings. Beautiful fountains would shoot out sprays of multi-colored waters.

The streets of our Utopian cities would be filled with music, soft and classical in some areas; rock in others. In other areas no recorded music would fill the air, but street musicians, and in other areas no music at all, just the sounds of birds, the rustling of leaves, and the chirping of crickets.

The skies of our Utopian cities would be free of pollution. The waters would run crystal clear. Parks and green spaces within the cities would never be closed by curfew. It would be possible to see the stars illuminate the Heavens at night even within the cities. The sunsets would be spectacular.

Fuller suggests that we could restore the great cities and buildings of yesteryear and send back to them all their treasures now scattered over the Earth in museums and private collections.

And so our Utopian cities would be humane, in balance with Nature, and highly livable.

TIME ZONES

Our Utopia could establish 'time zones' where people could live their lives as was done in various periods of the past: Zones of cave life, of the American colonial period, Old and New

Testament time zones, ancient Greece, etc. 'Wild West' areas might even be restored and maintained. Here adults of similar inclination could have real shoot—em-outs with one another, among themselves without harming
Society.

And to these time zones we would be able to send our children and ourselves in order to view past history and past accomplishments. Of particular interest should be this period we are living in today. A period when there is so much strife, war, and confusion, but yet an era of so much hope and revitalization. This will be a period when so many people are becoming aware of our Utopian promise and Utopian future. But in the future who would like to consider living in such a time zone and who would even bother to want to visit?

THE FAILURE OF POLITICS IN TODAY'S WORLD

According to Buckminster Fuller, all the metals that were ever mined and put to use are invested in structures and machines that even if operated at full capacity, would only take care of 44% of humanity. The rate at which new metals have been found and mined is far slower than the rate of increase of human population. If we should freeze the world's design standards at their present levels the renaming 56% of humanity, our world's population majority, is doomed to a premature demise, and to want and suffering en route to an early death.

"There is nothing," says Fuller, "that politics, per se, can do to alter that condition." Only a design revolution can change the "fundamental of humanity overnight from failure to comprehensive, world around, human success."

All politics can do is take from some and give to others. Politics cannot increase our overall quantity of goods so that all can enjoy abundance. Only technology can do that. 'Politics', just divides.

Fuller suggests:

Take away the power lines and the machinery from the world's industrialized countries and within six months more than two billion people will starve to death.

Take away the politicians and send them in a rocket to the sun, but make no alterations to our industrial machine, and suffering on Earth from starvation and disease will not increase, but the World will, in fact, probably get along much better.

The basic problem of governments is that if they have to choose between weapon development and environmental development, governments always seem to give priority to weaponry. Government channels the best minds into warfare rather than into social progress.

Even the democratic form of government is not keeping up with the changes necessary to preserve and bring about a truly meaningful life. In the United States it has been the 'democratically' elected Congressmen and Senators who voted to go along with several 'democratically' elected presidents' ideas to wage war on Southeast Asian countries. It is these same Congressmen and

Senators who continually vote for larger military budgets year after year. It is these same legislators who vote down meaningful measures to allocate money for social and environmental reform.

A person attempting to choose representatives to 'represent' him or her in the legislative arena is really up against it. First of all, both major political parties represent the same 'big money', status—quo interests. Both parties are tied to yesterday's scarcity, not-enough-to-go-around, assumptions. Many politicians will 'sell' their votes or allow themselves to be persuaded by the highest bidder. Massive election campaign expenses mean the need for rich and therefore demanding supporters.

We should not expect today's traditional politicians to find solutions to our present problems. They are all too closely specialized in their interests. They are too closely tied to nations and power trips and nationalism and false notions as to how to distribute the Earth's wealth. Politicians, like all specialists, are bound to human extinction, not life. They have too small a picture. They are not concerned with the whole. No, we must develop alternatives to today's tradition-bound politicians.

Recently, Detroit, the city wherein I lived, had a primary for nine City Council positions. One hundred and twenty-seven people ran for these nine positions. How was I, or anyone, for that matter, to know which nine of these 127 would do the 'best' job? Politicians have a tendency to say one thing now and do something else later, or else do nothing at all. Most people vote the way they do because of ethnic considerations, 'name' candidates, and the amount of publicity generated by the respective candidates' public relations firms.

But that doesn't mean, in conclusion, that a 'new' political movement based on honesty, technological and ecological awareness and 'One Earth Nationhood' couldn't bring about fantastic movement toward our Utopia. Later in the book we will consider the viability of an 'Earth Party.'

GOVERNMENT IN OUR UTOPIA

In our Utopia we shall move, from "the administration of people" to "the administration of things."

Henry David Thoreau, in his famous and still meaningful essay, *Civil Disobedience*', wrote:

"I heartily accept the motto; 'That government is best which governs least'; and I should like to see it acted up to more rapidly and systematically." Carried out, it finally amounts to this, which also I believe; 'That government is best which governs not at all'; and when men are prepared for it, that will be the kind of government which they will have.

In our future society, with the ending of war and with generous distribution of material goods, almost all of the functions of government will have disappeared.

In our Utopia there might be less need for fixed rules or laws. These change as people change. Most legal questions would certainly be abolished with the ending of scarcity, poverty, and capitalist and communist economics. Many years ago, about 600 B.C., Lao Tzu, the founder of a religion known as Taoism, wrote in his book '*The Way of Life*':

"When people lost sight of the way to live came codes of love and honesty. Learning came, charity came, hypocrisy took charge; when differences weakened family ties came benevolent fathers and dutiful sons, and when lands were disrupted and misgoverned came ministers commended as loyal."

As people regain the 'way to live,' the "Tao", as Lao Tzu called it, there should be less need for laws. We would not need policemen or soldiers. We'll all gain our heritage as Earth People, 'riders on the Spaceship Earth together'.

As Buckminster Fuller has observed, "Life tends to behave very well when it has the right environment." He says that we should not worry about reforming humankind. All we have to do is improve the environment, and humankind will improve itself.

CRIMINALS AND PRISONS

Persons who are in prisons all over the world today for political crimes would be released. The questions they struggled over: resistance to the draft, taxation, liberation of their native lands, and inequities in wealth, would be settled as we move towards our Utopia.

Persons who are in prisons because of "economic"

crimes, robbery and the like, might also be
released, as the causes for their imprisonment
will likewise have disappeared.

The persons in prison who have actually
committed crimes of willful violence and those
that are judged to be psychotic would be treated
as best we can through extensive reorientation and
reeducation to our Utopian Society's new norms. If
they are able to be cured and to really understand
the errors of their past ways -- they could be
released. If they could not be cured or
reoriented, they would stay in the institutions
which we would set up to house them. These
institutions would be humane but also secure. In
no sense would these people be allowed the freedom
to go out into society to again create havoc.

THE ADMINISTRATION OF THINGS

We will set up an administration of 'functional
organizations'. This administration will be viewed
as technological project coordinators rather than
political problem solvers. There is no reason why
such things as sewage treatment, street
cleaning, recreational programs, generation of
energy, etc., should be viewed in political terms,
and subject to political bickering and
mismanagement. These are totally functional
projects, just as mail delivery is considered
today.

Our Utopia would abandon today's
pre-technological social structure and install a
type of administration which is designed to
conform and grow within the changes which
technology has brought us in the way we lead our

lives.

When questions of public policy appear, they could be presented to the people by way of television.

Fuller suggests: Using computer wristwatches we could register our preferences on each issue, either by a yes/no vote, or by a preference scale of 0 to 10. The results would be registered and computed almost instantaneously. We will all be aware of what our fellow Earth Neighbors feel about any issue. We will be able to respond and interact with one another in a way so as to create, in the words of 16th century English political philosopher Jeremy Bentham, a method of calculating "the greatest happiness for the greatest number", the "maximizing of pleasure and the minimizing of pain."

Our Utopian Society would neither force nor threaten… "Love and Reason" would replace "Law and Order."

INNOVATIONS

Our Utopia would always be open to new concepts and change. Everyone would be encouraged to make suggestions as to how to improve things. Everyone would be free to criticize.

If you have an idea for a new product or service you would be encouraged to bring it forth. Your reward might not be in terms of money, but in the knowledge that you are contributing to the overall good of the Society.

Agencies of technologists, scientists,

philosophers, and regular Earth Folk would appraise your idea, and if they felt it to be beneficial, would see that it is put into operation. If one such agency does not approve, the idea could be considered by another. Change and improvement would be constant.

Fuller suggests that the data about new projects or proposed solutions to problems be fed into computers and that the computers could objectively indicate the best course of action.

Fuller says:

"A new physically uncompromised metaphysical initiative of unbiased integrity could unify the world. It would and probably will be provided by the utterly impersonal problem solutions of the computers. Only to their superhuman range of calculative capabilities can and may all political, scientific, and religious leaders face-savingly acquiesce."

Obviously, no matter which plan we may choose, we must be assured that red-tape is kept to a minimum and that bureaucracy never has a chance to raise its ugly head. We must not leave things to so-called 'experts' and then dismiss responsibility for them ourselves. Experts often have too narrow an interest or knowledge of things outside of their own expertise. They are not aware of the total picture.

In our Society, with the increase of educational standards, nothing would be out of reach of each citizen's understanding. There would be no 'secret negotiations', or the idea that we must not criticize because 'the government knows more than we do'.

We would guarantee that the 'people', not the 'state', controls our Society. But we also must be certain that the people are truly educated to all the alternatives by a life—long educational system.

FREEDOM AND RESPONSIBILITY

Freedom and Responsibility would be important aspects of our Utopia. People would be free of closed-circuit television cameras watching them and police agents spying on them. We would encourage trust and honesty among all people.

The theme of the book '*1984*', which describes a totally repressive state, would no longer remain a threat and a reality as it is in so many countries of the world today.

In our Utopia where most competitiveness has been removed, and everyone has equal amounts of the Earth's produce, and where positive values are being taught instead of negative ones; crime would likely disappear and so would violence. People would be responsible for their own behavior.

People would be self-regulating. We would all flourish under freedom, and sexism, racism, nationalism, and age chauvinism, would disappear forever.

PERFECT SOCIETY: PERFECT INDIVIDUALS

A society moving toward perfection will produce

perfect individuals… just as individuals moving toward perfection will, in turn, produce a perfect society.

Today we do not have perfect society, but we do have many individuals who are moving toward improvement in their own lives. It is through these people, people like you and me, people who are willing to question and to dream; that our Utopia will emerge. Indeed, we are the hope of our future.

Some people think that the love which Jesus Christ talked about was only for 'long ago' or 'far away'. In society as it is today, most people do not practice loving. When we do get our perfect society together, we will practice love… indeed, we will reach our perfected Society through LOVE.

In our future society we will offer and return 'good acts'. We will encourage the growth of positive feelings among Humankind. And we will help those who fear such feelings overcome their fears. We will establish a truly sharing community.

Perfection in body, perfection in mind; healing power; rejuvenating power; emotional balance, total Consciousness; total Beingness; these things will be ours in our perfected Utopia and in our perfected Consciousness.

Will life in our Utopia be boring?

Some people may ask: "With all this perfection with everything in our Utopia; won't life be boring?"

"Why must it be," we ask in return, "some calamity or unwelcome bother in order for life to be interesting?"

In our future society the best nature of humanity will come forth. Automation will free the automatons. We will all be able to pursue our highest creative energies. We will have time to do all the things we always wanted to do: art, travel, love making, meditating, education and even space travel throughout the Solar System.

As Buckminster Fuller writes in his book, "I Seem to Be a Verb":

When automation frees all workers, we will be able to ask, "What was it I was thinking that fascinated me so, before I was told I had to do something else in order to make a living?"

We need not be chained down to jobs, to bills, and to mortgages. Unlike growing plants, we are not stationary. We were given legs in order to explore our Universe. Could Heaven Here on Earth possibly be a bore?

HUMANS AS AN INTEGRAL FUNCTION OF THE UNIVERSE

We are not here by accident. We are here by design. We have purpose. We are life experiencing itself.

Buckminster Fuller, besides being a technologist, is also a philosopher. I would be remiss in this book if I did not try to convey some of his thoughts about his, and therefore our own, relationship to life and to the Universe. Perhaps his insights can help you as they have helped me.

Fuller writes:

"I live on Earth at present, and I don't know what I am. I know that I am not a category. I am not a thing — a noun, I seem to be a verb, an evolutionary process — an integral function of the universe."

When one thinks of Descartes, one recalls, "I think, therefore I am." With Bucky it's "I experience, whatever I am."

Fuller was saddened in 1922 by the death of his young daughter. The next five years were times of confusion for him. He was uncertain about his life and his future. Fran 1927 until 1929 he decided to observe silence and spend his time trying to figure himself out. He has said that he went back to thinking about all the things he had thought about and learned before he had decided to "earn a living." He went back to a childlike state, with eyes open to see and to understand.

"This is really where I started. I was not called an architect; I was not called anything. I was simply faced with the problem of organizing myself in a great many ways to pursue such a course. But I found it's actually possible for an individual to make first moves, and that these will incite various others.

"So I said to myself, 'If this gets anywhere, it's going to take 50 years and unless you're willing to spend 50 years, don't touch it. Because it's too important. It's too big and right. Don't flub this one, or you'll discourage a lot of others coming along."

In 1927 Bucky was seriously considering suicide. He was standing beside Lake Michigan ready to throw himself in; when in a dialogue with himself he turned his life around. His principal insight appears to have been that he possessed a remarkably diverse inventory of experiences. If he destroyed himself the experience would all perish too, and be lost to others whom it might benefit. He had no right to take it from them. "You do not have the right to eliminate yourself, you do not belong to you. You belong to the universe. The significance of you will forever remain obscure to you — but you may assume that you are fulfilling your significance if you apply yourself to converting all your experience to the highest advantage of others"

HOW DO WE GET THERE?

Optimistically speaking, the longer we survive as a species on this planet, each day, week, year; the better are our chances for long term survival. Each day we are developing the new technologies and the new ideas to correct the ecological, social, and economic problems that we face.

Inventors must keep inventing.

Technologists must keep applying technology.

You and I must continue to learn, question, explore.

Keep exposing yourself to new ideas -- new

horizons. We must read science and technology books. Read novels about Utopia – Edward Bellamy's *'Looking Backward'*; and *'Island'* by Aldous Huxley are great ones. You could also read anti-utopian novels which indicate how bad life could be if we don't get ourselves together: George Orwell's *'1984'*, and Aldous Huxley's *'Brave New World'*. An interesting note in that Huxley wrote *'Brave New World'* at an earlier part of his life. Later, toward the end of his life, he became more optimistic about our human potential and wrote *'Island'*. Both are excellent reads.

You can begin to tell your friends about the prospects of Utopia. Explain to them how Utopia is both possible and desirable. Tell than we're all 'Earth People' and a 'One Earth Nation'. Turn them on to Buckminster Fuller. Acknowledge and proclaim your own Earth Citizenship.

You see, each one of us has a 'Universe of Experiences' which we can share with our fellow beings. We must discuss with one another. We must dream with one another. We must talk with one another.

Many persons within society face the major problem of resistance to new ideas and to change. But the measure of growth is the willingness to change and to grow and to seek out new knowledge, even accepting that which was previously unacceptable. Sometimes we wait for stresses and crises to force us to open our minds to new ideas, inventions, attitudes, and actions. Our resistance to change is primarily due to our fears and our lack of knowing who to believe about claims and promises of what would happen if we did things differently. There are answers to our problems.

But we won't answer these problems until they are so severe that we are forced by them to become much more open-minded than we are now.

Society is not suffering from what it doesn't know. It is suffering from what it does know, but refuses to do because too many of us have our minds closed to new and better ideas and ways. But this is good.

This is what is causing situations to be more and more critical with every passing week. Indeed, the crises are working wonderfully. More and more persons are ready to listen to new ideas and to try to lead the public into different and better ways of doing things.

Each day more and more people are 'turning on' to Ecology and to the possibilities of One Earth Nationhood. They are becoming better educated and more aware. This is allowing them to ask new questions and to think of new alternatives. Ecology may well be the Great Common Denominator which will unite all Humankind. Ecological concerns will provide the knowledge of and incentive for how we humans can live and interact in balance with our environment.

WE CANNOT AFFORD ANYTHING ELSE; BUT TO MAKE OUR WORLD WORK!

In the midst of World War II a young girl lived hidden away in an attic, concealed from the Nazis. She and her family were eventually found and the girl, whose name was Anne Frank, perished in one of the Nazi concentration camps.

While in hiding she composed a diary which was later published as '*The Diary of a Young Girl*'. Here is one of its most hopeful and beautiful passages:

"I keep my ideals, because in spite of everything I still believe that people are really good at heart. I simply can't build up my hopes on a foundation consisting of confusion, misery, and death. I can feel the sufferings of millions and yet, if I look up into the heavens, I think that it will all come right, that this cruelty too will end, and that peace and tranquility will return again."

EARTH CENTERS

As a further means toward achieving Earth Union, Ecological Balance, and increased Consciousness; 'Earth Centers' could be set up. These would be buildings which would be utilized for meetings and classes in ecological and technological awareness. People would come together to work out programs to educate themselves and to spread the 'good word'.

The first of such Centers emerged in Hamtramck, Michigan, a suburb of Detroit. It opened on the first day of Spring; March, 20, 1974. It is supported by dues, donations, and Earth Industries, such as natural foods, vegetarian restaurants, a health food store, a ballroom, and a bakery. Hopefully as word of the success of this first Earth Center spreads more centers would develop Earthwide. The Hamtramck Earth Center places particular emphasis on Growth Movements and has classes in Yoga, tai chi, organic gardening, modern dance, and many other things as time passes.

The Earth Center Address is:
11464 Mitchell
Hamtramck, Michigan 48212

{Author Note: The Earth Center died throughout the Summer months of 1975. In its short life it had positive effects on hundreds of people. The building now houses a Zen Center.}

EARTH PARTY:
THE FAILURE OF THE UNITED NATIONS

The United Nations Organization was set up after World War II as a means of creating world peace and world unity. Its success in these areas has, unfortunately, been rather limited.

Perhaps the major reason that the UN has not worked is that it is a top—down organization set up by countries and participation of ordinary citizens is not allowed. Countries, like most institutions, are on their own ego-power trips. They do not want to give up any of their so-called sovereign powers to any central entity.

What is needed is a new movement of the Earth's peoples independent of countries to establish the One Earth Nation and the Earth Utopia. This movement must be organized from the bottom—up by ordinary people who would then exert influence on the societies and governments of their respective countries. This movement could be called the Earth Party. In all countries around the globe, wherever it is democratically possible, the Earth Party

would nominate and run candidates. These
candidates would campaign more on a party basis
than on an individual one. They would campaign on
the prospects of One Earth Nationhood and
Ecological and Technological Awareness.

This Earth Party must singularly strive to
overcome the pitfalls of other political events
described earlier in this book. This could be done
by the candidates and the Party having a working
knowledge of the Utopian alternatives to our
present day chaos. The Earth Party would act as
both an educational forum as well as seriously
attempting to elect its candidates to public
office.

Imagine the effects of such an Earth Party
electing government officials in the United States,
Canada, Great Britain, Western Europe Israel,
Japan, Costa Rica, Argentina, etc. All would say
the same thing: That we're all brothers and sisters
on this, our planet Earth, and that we can live in
Ecological Harmony. Fantastic! And in those
countries where it is not possible to run
candidates in a democratic electoral process,
perhaps discussion groups could be set up. The
call for Freedom would have international effects.
A suggestion by Fuller is appropriate here:

"Society is full of this horrible thing, fear, and
when society is fearful, it gets panicky and does
stupid things. So don't do things just to defy or
make people fearful. Do things to give them
confidence. Don't do things which invite opposition.
Do things which invite support. Try to think
clearly, and you will find answers for your
problems. Very shortly, society will be in enough
trouble to want them."

CONCLUSION

One of the most beautiful selections from the Old
Testament is "The Prophecy of Peace" from the
prophet Micah 4: 1-4;

"In the end of days it shall come to pass that the
mountain of the Lord's house shall be established
at the top of the mountains, and it shall be
exalted above the hills… And He shall judge
between many peoples, and shall decide
concerning mighty nations afar off; and they shall
beat their swords into plowshares, and their spears
into pruning hooks; nations shall not lift up
sword against nation, neither shall they learn war
any more. But they shall sit everyone under their
fig tree, and none shall make then afraid."

Murray Bookchin has written: "We cannot be
extravagant enough in releasing the imagination
of humankind."

So let's get started on the road.

Also By

'MARVIN MARVIN' SUROWITZ

A World That Works For Everybody:
Visions Of Utopia; Buckminster Fuller And Me
https://www.createspace.com/3462191

A Survival Guide To The War On Drugs:
How We Can Win It; How We Can End It
https://www.createspace.com/3467244

Hemp / Marijuana / Cannabis:
God's Sacrament; The Holy Bible; And You!
https://www.createspace.com/3471621

Student Evaluations Of Professor 'Marvin Marvin'
Surowitz: Students From Marvin's Classes
Throughout The Years
https://www.createspace.com/3489505

Celebrate The Blessing Of God's Word:
To Lose Weight And Love Life
https://www.createspace.com/3473394

You may also order kindle versions from Amazon.

profsurowitz@hotmail.com

S.J. FLECK

Last Night I Had A Dream: It Was A Sound Machine

Search for Title or Author on Amazon.

stevejfleck@gmail.com

Professor
'Marvin Marvin' Surowitz